Changing the Indian Economy

ELSEVIER

ASIAN STUDIES SERIES

Series Editor: Professor Chris Rowley,
Kellogg College, Oxford University, UK;
Cass Business School, City, University of London, UK
(email: chris.rowley@kellogg.ox.ac.uk)

Elsevier is pleased to publish this major Series of books entitled Asian Studies: Contemporary Issues and Trends. The Series Editor is Professor Chris Rowley of Cass Business School, City University, London, UK and Department of International Business and Asian Studies, Griffith University, Australia.

Asia has clearly undergone some major transformations in recent years and books in the Series examine this transformation from a number of perspectives: economic, management, social, political and cultural. We seek authors from a broad range of areas and disciplinary interests covering, for example, business/management, political science, social science, history, sociology, gender studies, ethnography, economics and international relations, etc.

Importantly, the Series examines both current developments and possible future trends. The Series is aimed at an international market of academics and professionals working in the area. The books have been specially commissioned from leading authors. The objective is to provide the reader with an authoritative view of current thinking.

New authors: we would be delighted to hear from you if you have an idea for a book. We are interested in both shorter, practically orientated publications (45,000+words) and longer, theoretical monographs (75,000-100,000 words). Our books can be single, joint or multi-author volumes. If you have an idea for a book, please contact the publishers or Professor Chris Rowley, the Series Editor.

Dr Glyn Jones
Email: g.jones.2@elsevier.com

Professor Chris Rowley
Email: chris.rowley@kellogg.ox.ac.uk

Changing the Indian Economy

Renewal, Reform and Revival

Edited by

RAMA P. KANUNGO
Newcastle University London, London, United Kingdom

CHRIS ROWLEY
Kellogg College, Oxford University, United Kingdom, and Cass Business School, City, University of London, United Kingdom

ANURAG N. BANERJEE
University of Durham, Durham, United Kingdom

ELSEVIER

Elsevier
Radarweg 29, PO Box 211, 1000 AE Amsterdam, Netherlands
The Boulevard, Langford Lane, Kidlington, Oxford OX5 1GB, United Kingdom
50 Hampshire Street, 5th Floor, Cambridge, MA 02139, United States

Notices
Knowledge and best practice in this field are constantly changing. As new research and experience
broaden our understanding, changes in research methods, professional practices, or medical treatment
may become necessary.

Practitioners and researchers must always rely on their own experience and knowledge in evaluating and
using any information, methods, compounds, or experiments described herein. In using such information
or methods they should be mindful of their own safety and the safety of others, including parties for
whom they have a professional responsibility.

To the fullest extent of the law, neither the Publisher nor the authors, contributors, or editors, assume
any liability for any injury and/or damage to persons or property as a matter of products liability,
negligence or otherwise, or from any use or operation of any methods, products, instructions, or ideas
contained in the material herein.

Library of Congress Cataloging-in-Publication Data
A catalog record for this book is available from the Library of Congress

British Library Cataloguing-in-Publication Data
A catalogue record for this book is available from the British Library

ISBN: 978-0-08-102005-0

For information on all Elsevier publications visit our website at
https://www.elsevier.com/books-and-journals

www.elsevier.com • www.bookaid.org

Publisher: Jonathan Simpson
Acquisition Editor: Glyn Jones
Editorial Project Manager: Charlotte Rowley
Production Project Manager: Poulouse Joseph
Designer: Matthew Limbert

Typeset by Thomson Digital

CONTENTS

LIST OF CONTRIBUTORS

Anurag N. Banerjee
University of Durham, Durham, United Kingdom

Nilanjan Banik
Bennett University, India

T.A. Bhavani
Institute of Economic Growth, Delhi, India

Suraksha Gupta
Newcastle University London, London, United Kingdom

William Joe
Institute of Economic Growth, Delhi, India

Abhishek Kumar
Research Scholar, Central University of Gujarat, Gujarat, India

Rama P. Kanungo
Newcastle University London, London, United Kingdom

Geethanjali Nataraj
Indian Institute of Public Administration (IIPA), New Delhi, India

Bibhas Saha
Durham University Business School, Durham, United Kingdom

Shreyosi Saha
University of Cambridge, Cambridge, United Kingdom

Seema Sangita
TERI School of Advanced Studies, New Delhi, India

Kavita Sharma
University of Delhi, New Delhi, India

Anjali Tandon
Institute for Studies in Industrial Development (ISID), New Delhi, India

Gipson Varghese
National Skill Development Corporation, New Delhi, India

PREFACE

India has witnessed a series of unprecedented socioeconomic changes over the past 5 years that have morphed the Indian economic landscape. India is using reformist economic processes for its renewal and growth, and the Indian economy has currently experienced a series of reforms and renewed several existing frameworks. Reformed financial planning for financial literacy via digital finance, the implementation of international statutory accounting and banking standards and financial transparency leading to the professionalism of the Indian financial sector are many facets of such changes. India has undertaken several socioeconomic liberalisations including demonetisation, digital-payment systems and a unified taxation system. However, the ability of these benefits to reach the less privileged in India remains elusive. In addition, the gap between industrialised countries and emerging countries (i.e. India) is one of the key challenges facing the Indian government.

Under renewed economic initiatives, effective resource allocation and parsimonious governance could improve the economic growth of India. Despite several economic measures, the process of renewal has not been fully achieved in India. There are several underlying factors that have contributed to the lack of fulfilment of certain aspects of reform and renewal. Beyond the historic trends of governmental reforms, it is not clear what differences these reforms bring. How could the government balance these changes to optimise reforms? The trends in the Indian economy and the timeliness of the government's response to these changes remains inconclusive. The recent government has demonstrated overreaching efforts to reform and renew the economic system; however, these reforms are not making desired changes at the ground level.

This book discusses the current scene and elucidates how different measures of reform have affected the diverse aspects of the Indian economy. The book recounts how India has a strong potential to grow amidst the diverse economic reforms and changing governance.

Rama P. Kanungo
Newcastle University, London, United Kingdom

CHAPTER 1

Political Economy of Resources and Infrastructure in India

Anurag N. Banerjee*, Nilanjan Banik**
*University of Durham, Durham, United Kingdom
**Bennett University, India

1 PROBLEMS WITH LAND ACQUISITION

Obtaining land for infrastructure or for the building industry is a real problem and can slow down growth. Table 1.1 shows that India lags behind other South Asian countries (with similar levels of economic development), not only in terms of per capita income but also with respect to other key development indicators such as electricity, water and sanitation. In India, obtaining land for infrastructure and the building industry remains a thorny issue.

Analysis by TMP Systems found that out of 73,000 commercial projects across eight different countries, over 93% of projects were inhabited. When analysing 262 land tenure cases in 30 countries, the study found consistent material impacts of unclear land rights obstructing the building of new infrastructures, including dams, roads, ports and electricity supplies.[a] Therefore obtaining land with a clear title is an issue.

The story is no different in India. With limited government resources, there is a need for public–private partnerships (PPPs) to develop world-class infrastructure and service sector operations. The provision of hassle-free and cheap land to private companies for developing infrastructure is an essential component for this to happen. Investment risks posed by insecure and unclear land rights are responsible for holding back investment in infrastructure. At the other extreme, farmers and human rights activists complain that they are on the receiving end, with middlemen cornering the bulk of the profit.

---

[a] For more on this see: https://news.mongabay.com/2015/10/failure-to-engage-local-communities-is-costinginvestors-big-money-according-to-a-new-analysis/.

Changing the Indian Economy
http://dx.doi.org/10.1016/B978-0-08-102005-0.00001-0

Table 1.1 Income and Infrastructural Indicators

Indicator	India	South Asia	Lower Middle Income Countries
GNI per capita, Atlas method (current USD) in 2016	1670	1611	2077.69
Access to electricity (% of population) in 2014	79.16	80.05	79.53
Access to improved water source (% of population) in 2015	94.1	92.37	89.18
Access to improved sanitation facilities (% of population) in 2015	39.6	44.77	52.22
Electricity Power Consumption (kWh per capita) in 2014	805.59	707.55	769.05

Source: World Development Indicators (2017), World Bank.

2 IMPACT ON INDUSTRY

A study examining 1660 judgements delivered in the Punjab and Haryana High Court between 2009 and 2011 demonstrated how farmers are deprived (Singh, 2012). The study showed that the average government compensation was approximately one-fourth of the market value of the land. Moreover, most of the land procured for building infrastructure was used for commercial purposes [i.e. real estate and special economic zones (SEZs)]. Developers from Noida (Uttar Pradesh) and Gurgaon (Haryana) in the National Capital Region (NCR) have made fortunes. For example, in 2006, approximately 5000 farmers from five villages received a notice that the Haryana Urban Development Authority would be acquiring 638 acres of their land. The land was acquired in 2009, and the farmers received compensation of INR 16 lakhs per acre, an amount they felt was far below the market price. Sales of land in the same area in 2015 fetched up to INR 22 crore per acre. The farmers are now demanding that they are fairly compensated, as much of the reason for the skyrocketing land price is the development of commercial and residential properties in the region.[b]

A report from the Comptroller and Auditor General of India provided an account of the misuse of land in Special Economic Zone (SEZ). It concludes that 'land appears to be the most crucial and attractive component of the scheme. Out of 45,635.63 ha of land notified in the country for SEZ purposes, operations commenced in only 28,488.49 ha of land'.[c] It also added that '5402.22 ha of land was de-notified and diverted for commercial purposes in several cases'. Many tracts of these lands were acquired invoking the 'public purpose' clause, which is used for developing infrastructure. Data from the Ministry of Statistics and Programme Implementation show that more than 82% of projects suffered delays. This was true even under the 1894 Land Acquisition Act, which contained a notorious 'urgency clause' that permitted land acquisition without any scrutiny or hindrance.

Perhaps to invoke transparency and to ensure that the farmers got the right price, the government introduced the Right to Fair Compensation and Transparency in Land Acquisition, Rehabilitation and Resettlement (LARR) Act (2013). This was an amendment to the original Land Acquisition Act (1894). The LARR Act, which was passed on 29 August 2013, stated that to procure land to establish a private industry, consent must be taken from 80% of landowners and people on government assigned land[d]; however, the consent of people who depend on the land for their livelihood is not required. For PPP projects, consent must be taken from 70% of landowners and people on government assigned land. The government retains the ownership of land in PPP projects. The time limit for acquiring land was set to 1 year. Provisions were added to ensure that speculators who purchase land at a low price do not benefit. Tenants living off sharecropping above a certain period also receive compensation.

[b] Namrata Kohli (2015). NCR farmers claiming back their land, demanding compensation. Hindustan Times. Available at: http://www.hindustantimes.com/india/ncr-farmers-claiming-back-their-land-demandingcompensation/story-RCq75b69r7QXKHtdfOw2RO.html.

[c] Comptroller and Auditor General of India (2014), Report Number 21, Government of India, New Delhi. Available at: http://www.cag.gov.in/sites/default/files/audit_report_files/Union_Performance_Dept_Revenue_Indirect_Taxes_Special_Economic_Zones_SEZs_21_2014_chapter_8.pdf.

[d] Land Acquisition, Rehabilitation and Resettlement Bill, 77-2011 (LARR, 2011). Available at: http://164.100.24.219/BillsTexts/LSBillTexts/asintroduced/land%20acquisition%2077%20of%202011.pdf.

It is the compensation that is important for farmers. Policies for releasing agricultural land for nonagricultural purposes should be designed in a fashion that allows farmers to remain as stakeholders. Farmers do not want to give away land as it provides them with collateral and helps to sustain their income. The land acquisition process cannot be left to the market as the transaction costs would be much higher, particularly when the buyer has to negotiate with numerous small-scale sellers and land records are spotty. However, it should not be left to the government either, as the price the government offers is arbitrary and may not reflect the true price. The government also acquires land citing a public purpose and subsequently transfers it to their partner companies. Postacquisition companies use the land for real estate and other commercial purposes and make huge profits. Examples including the housing projects under PPPs for the Taj and the Ganga expressway projects and hospitality projects associated with Delhi and Mumbai airports. The price often increases to more than the market price because of third-party intervention, such as land brokers with strong political connections. These land brokers typically procure land in bulk before the start of the project. Therefore even if the farmers willingly gave their land to the government or land brokers before the start of the project, they may start to feel agitated when they discover that the price of the land skyrocketed after the start of the project. This agitation was seen in farmers in Greater Noida, Uttar Pradesh, in May 2011. Those who willingly gave land began to feel left out or cheated as the price of land increased several-fold upon completion of the Yamuna Expressway (connecting Delhi and Agra).

Given how the land market operates in India, the market price is not an adequate anchor for compensation nor an efficient use of scarce resources, notwithstanding its pro-poor reference. Bardhan (2011) put forward the concept of an independent quasi-judicial regulatory authority to oversee land acquisitions.[e] Many parts of the economy (i.e. telecom and the stock markets) already have established regulatory provisions. Land is an economic sector that could benefit from a quasi-judicial body. Land transfer, administration of compensation and settlement must be handled by a quasi-judicial authority that is independent of political influence but subject to periodic legislative review. According to Ghatak and Ghosh (2011), this problem can

[e] Land Acquisition: Currently A Major Stumbling Block for Development Policy. In: Development Outreach, World Bank. Available at. http://eml.berkeley.edu/~webfac/bardhan/papers/WBILand%20Acquisition.pdf.

be solved through land auction, which covers both the project area and surrounding farmland. If properly implemented, this procedure will allow farmers to choose compensation as either cash or land and to determine their own price instead of leaving it to the government.

The bottom line is that farmers must be made stakeholders to prevent agitation and to allow the procurement of land without any trouble. Farmers can be given some land in developed form (permission to build); for instance, one political leader in Uttar Pradesh, Mayawati, has promised to give 13% of land in developed form. Another method is to offer jobs, which is something what the Chief Minister of Gujarat, Narendra Modi, is promising. For example, if a factory is built on the procured land, one member of the family will get a job in the factory.

3 IMPACT ON THE POWER SECTOR

Energy demand in India is growing at a rapid rate, rising from 450 million tonnes of oil equivalent (toe) in 2000 to 900 million toe in 2015. This is expected to increase further to 1500 million toe in 2030. India also consumes approximately 1100 billion units of electricity every year. Residential and commercial buildings consume around 37% of total electricity consumption. A total of 1 billion m^2 of new commercial buildings are expected to be added by 2030.

It is noteworthy that the power sector was the first infrastructure sector that saw opening up to private participation and yet it is the sector that has encountered the greatest difficulty. Private investment in the power sector has fallen substantially short of expectations. The basic strategy was to invite private participation in the generation segment, with independent power projects (IPPs) expected to sell power to the State Electricity Boards (SEBs). However, the reluctance of state governments to tackle the basic issues of power theft and inadequate tariffs led to the bankruptcy of SEBs and prevented the financial closure of IPPs. Attempts to bypass these basic problems through stratagems such as escrow arrangements and central government guarantees have also not worked. In addition, the protracted and acrimonious negotiations over the Dabhol power project in Maharashtra highlighted the political risks of IPPs and are sufficient to put off any new investment. This has led to the current issues related to land acquisition.

The problem with obtaining land for building power plants persists to date. In January 2017, violent protests erupted in the South 24 Pargana district of West Bengal, India. Villagers were opposed to the Power

Grid Corporation of India Limited (PGCIL) building a power substation in their area. PGCIL stated that they wanted to construct a 400/220 kV gas-insulated substation to supply power from Farakka in West Bengal to Kahalgaon in Bihar; however, the locals told a different story. They alleged that the land has previously been forcibly obtained by one faction of the All India Trinamool Congress (TMC), which is the ruling party in West Bengal. This group, whose leader is Arabul Islam, had already sold these forcibly-acquired lands to real estate developers. When the PGCIL attempted to build a power substation at the behest of the state government, it became a member of this fall-out group that was instigating the villagers to go against the state.[f] In fact, the present Member of Parliament for the region, Abdur Rajjak Molla, shares an acrimonious relationship with Arabul Islam which makes things worse. To save face, TMC party bosses told the media that the problems with land acquisition in the region had nothing to do with the internal feud between TMC workers but happened with support from the Maoist group.

3.1 Impact of Mining

When it comes to mining, the government needs land for rehabilitation. The problem has been that of rehabilitation of the tribes and villagers. India has an abundance of minerals, especially iron ore, bauxite, mica and coal. India is the third largest producer of iron ore, the fifth largest producer of bauxite and one of the largest producers of mica in the world. It has been alleged that the mining companies do not appropriately compensate local communities. This is an example of the resource curse, where capital-intensive mining companies, whose primary objective is exporting, have little or no obligation to the local community.[g] In fact, mining is not performed efficiently by these companies, which has led to a natural resource deficit. In addition to importing two-thirds of its required oil, India is projected to overtake China as the world's largest coal importer in the next decade, even though China's coal consumption is currently over six-fold higher than India's. India has also slipped from being the third largest iron ore exporter to being at risk of becoming a net importer. India was also, until recently, the world's largest consumer and importer of gold. It is important to realise that

[f] The Telegraph (2017). Bhangar on boil again. Available at: https://www.telegraphindia. com/1170513/jsp/bengal/story_151340.jsp.

[g] The resource curse (also known as the paradox of plenty) refers to the failure of many resource-rich countries to benefit fully from their natural resource wealth and for governments in these countries to respond effectively to public welfare needs.

this natural-resource deficit is the primary source of the macroeconomic vulnerabilities that the country is grappling with. There are several problems that the government (both central and state) are trying to identify and solve.

India is losing natural resources inspite of having several progressive laws relating to forest lands, and tribal communities and their lands. There is the Forest Right Act (2006) and the Provisions of the Panchayats (Extension to Scheduled Areas) Act, which was enacted by the Government of India (GOI) to ensure self-governance through traditional Gram Sabhas for individuals living in the Scheduled Areas of India. However, there are allegations that these laws are not properly implemented, and that tribal communities are not consulted as to whether they would like to voluntarily give up their lands to the mining communities. This has led to social unrest and the government occasionally rejecting the requests of mining companies. For example, the GOI blocked Vedanta's bid to build a mine in Orissa in 2010 after considering the interests of the 8000-strong Dongria Kondh community. The Dongria Kondh's determination to protect the Niyamgiri Hills from Vedanta paid off, despite the state government being complicit in the USD 2 billion project. The community campaigned against the mining project for almost a decade amidst alleged intimidation by paramilitary police and local goons. The GOI and the supreme court bucked the trend of siding with the industry and defended the rights of the Dongria Kondh community to their lands and livelihoods. The decision of the environment ministry to block Vedanta should serve as a warning to any company intent on extracting resources from tribal land without the informed consent of members.[h] The message is that if these progressive laws are implemented in spirit then tribal rights and environments can be protected. It is necessary to take a holistic approach to understanding the costs (ecological and the human cost of displacement) and benefits (profitability of the mining companies) of the projects related to mining and extraction. The impacts of India's resource curse could be lessened if the government approached existing laws as a means to achieve a just, democratic and ecologically-informed conversation.

In a recent landmark judgement, the Supreme Court of India imposed penalties of approximately INR 25,000 crores on illegal mining.[i] Two aspects of the verdict stand out: first, the verdict takes environmental law enforcement by the government and the judicial authority to a new high,

[h] https://www.theguardian.com/global-development/poverty-matters/2014/jan/14/india-rejection-vedanta-mine-victory-tribal-rights.
[i] For more on this see: http://judicialreforms.org/100-penalty-orissas-illegal-mining-sc-landmark-case/.

which is a very strong deterrent against such practices in the future; and second, the court ordered heavy expenditure for the welfare of tribal people in affected areas.

Conventionally, mining was only deemed to be illegal if ores were extracted without a mining lease. Under the mining law, the penalty was equal to the entire output from such an operation. However, once the lease was obtained, even if the mining operation ravaged forests, made the air unbreathable, degraded the environment and produced thousands of crores of profit, the penalty under the environment law was a laughable INR 50,000. This provided businesses with a strong incentive to start mining without waiting for green clearances (Table 1.2). However, under this current Supreme Court order, extracting minerals without the necessary green clearance should be deemed illegal, not just under the environmental law but also under the mining law that imposes back-breaking penalties for default. This means that even if a mining lease is obtained, any extraction without forestry and environmental clearance is illegal and the state must recover the value of the entire output from the defaulter: this is a welcome move.

The Supreme Court judgement resulted in a 19% decrease in mining in Orissa, from 221 mines in 2009–10 to 179 mines in 2013–14. However, the judgement has generally been good for the Indian mining industry, which increased by 21% over the same period. Table 1.3 and Fig. 1.1 show that the better-governed states have shown increased mining activities. The regression between the governance index and the growth rate of mining activities shows that there is a significant positive correlation between governance and mining. This indicates that governance of the mining sector has a direct impact on the investment in resource-rich states. Investors monitor the governance of the mining sector in each state and reward better performance

Table 1.2 Investment in subsectors of the Indian economy

Subsector	Project count	Total investment (USD million)
Water and sewerage	16	624
Natural gas	5	1,015
Airports	7	5,111
Railways	8	7,826
Ports	39	8,745
Roads	388	73,606
ICT	37	100,231
Electricity	381	143,476

Source: www.worldbank.org data from 2016.

Table 1.3 Governance and mining activities in Indian states

State	Total mineral mines		Growth rate (%)	Governance index 2011
	2009–10	2013–14		
Andhra Pradesh	456	660	44.74	0.57
Arunachal Pradesh	1	1		
Assam	11	6	−45.45	0.5
Bihar	6	5	−16.67	0.29
Chhattisgarh	152	203	33.55	0.5
Goa	75	69	−8.00	
Gujarat	446	464	4.04	0.65
Haryana	0	1		0.58
Himachal Pradesh	26	21	−19.23	0.53
Jammu & Kashmir	11	7	−36.36	
Jharkhand	299	233	−22.07	0.3
Karnataka	233	187	−19.74	0.56
Kerala	30	49	63.33	0.59
Madhya Pradesh	287	364	26.83	0.49
Maharashtra	158	168	6.33	0.54
Manipur	0	0		
Meghalaya	9	14	55.56	
Odisha	221	179	−19.00	0.34
Rajasthan	289	556	92.39	0.59
Sikkim	0	0		0.31
Tamil Nadu	175	355	102.86	0.61
Uttar Pradesh	25	19	−24.00	0.29
Uttarakhand	34	17	−50.00	0.35
West Bengal	112	121	8.04	0.5
Total	**3056**	**3699**	**21.08**	

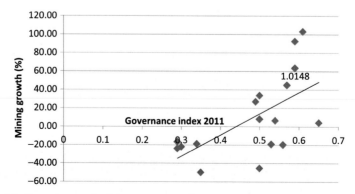

Figure 1.1 *Growth rate of mining versus good governance in 2010–14.*

with a lower cost of capital by lowering the risk. This shows that well-managed mining projects offer an opportunity to transform resource wealth into sustainable development in India.

3.2 Impact on Connectivity

Obtaining land has also been a problem for expanding physical infrastructure. India's transport sector is large and diverse and caters to the needs of 1.3 billion people. In 2017, the sector contributed approximately 6.5% of the nation's gross domestic product (GDP), with road transportation contributing the largest share. Good physical connectivity in urban and rural areas is essential for economic growth. Since the early 1990s, India's growing economy has witnessed a rise in demand for transport infrastructure and services (Table 1.4). For example, in 1990–92 there was only one private sector road project; however, this rose to 31 projects during 2014–16. There was no investment in ports and railways during 1991–92, but by 2014–16 this had risen to three new private sector investments in ports and one in the railway.

In the infrastructure space, it is a challenge to build urban infrastructure. Urban and rural India face a transport crisis that is characterised by high levels of congestion, noise, pollution, traffic-related fatalities and injuries that far exceed other developed countries. The main concern with developing a public transport system had been the disproportionate influence of personal vehicle manufacturers in cooperation with the newly emerging middle class.

In the case of the rural sector, which is constitutionally under the state governments, the GOI started the Pradhan Mantri Gram Sadak Yojana (PMGSY) as a one-time measure to reduce rural connectivity problems. However, there still appears to be a gap between road construction targets and actual completion of the work (Table 1.5). It also indicates that governance at the state level plays a role in the completion of projects despite the financial burden being shouldered by the GOI (Fig. 1.2). Thus the sector has not been able to keep pace with the rising demands and is

Table 1.4 Growth in the number of private infrastructure projects in India

Sector	Projects reaching financial closure	
	1990–92	2014–16
Electricity	3	60
Ports	0	3
Railways	0	1
Roads	1	31
Water and sewerage	0	2

Table 1.5 Rural roads between 2000–16 under PMGSY

State	Target length (km)	Completed length (km)	Governance index	Performance gap (%)
Andhra Pradesh	2,1695.30	1,3786.57	0.57	−36.45
Arunachal Pradesh	5,252.38	5,782.95		10.10
Assam	1,9848.00	16,500.33	0.5	−16.87
Bihar	60,123.00	44,027.05	0.29	−26.77
Chhattisgarh	32,632.00	27,180.51	0.5	−16.71
Goa	57.42	155.33		170.52
Gujarat	9,657.83	12,522.63	0.65	29.66
Haryana	4,464.86	5,567.01	0.58	24.69
Himachal Pradesh	13,206.40	12,662.26	0.53	−4.12
Jammu And Kashmir	12,433.60	7,344.08		−40.93
Jharkhand	21,818.07	16,112.35	0.3	−26.15
Karnataka	13,238.40	18,533.50	0.56	40.00
Kerala	4,457.23	2,917.81	0.59	−34.54
Madhya Pradesh	64,825.00	67,346.63	0.49	3.89
Maharashtra	21,916.33	25,619.22	0.54	16.90
Manipur	4,460.61	5,671.46		27.15
Meghalaya	1,985.96	1,596.17		−19.63
Mizoram	2,355.87	2,643.16		12.19
Nagaland	2,682.55	3,483.87		29.87
Odisha	49,384.00	41,426.94	0.34	−16.11
Punjab	7,210.99	7,669.72	0.59	6.36
Rajasthan	47,438.00	62,803.72	0.31	32.39
Sikkim	2,554.91	3,289.72		28.76
Tamil Nadu	12,110.58	14,213.28	0.61	17.36
Tripura	5,091.41	3,973.61		−21.95
Uttar Pradesh	50,944.00	50,610.64	0.29	−0.65
Uttarakhand	10,316.03	8,101.82	0.35	−21.46
West Bengal	27,584.21	23,511.31	0.5	−14.77
Telangana	1,725.00	9,962.00		477.51
Total	**531455.94**	**515015.65**		**96.9**

PMGSY, Pradhan Mantri Gram Sadak Yojana.
Source: http://omms.nic.in/.

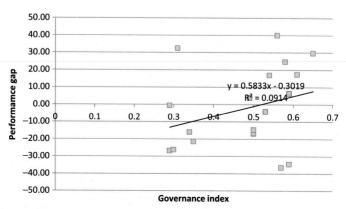

Figure 1.2 *Performance gap in constructing rural roads and governance.*

proving to be a drag on the economy. Major improvements in the sector are required to support the country's continued economic growth and to reduce poverty.

The quality of highways will improve substantially in the coming years. The government has made rapid progress in implementing the National Highway Development Project. There have been some efficiency gains in ports through the privatisation of port services and berths. The telecom sector has perhaps seen the most significant development, as greater clarity in regulatory and policy environments has accelerated activities and expanded coverage. Several private operators are already active in this market and are raising funds through bond financing. Tariffs in the telecom sector have reduced thanks to deregulation, competition and technology. In no sector of the economy have prices fallen as fast as in the telecom sector.

India has a coastline spanning 7516.6 km, comprising 5422.6 km of mainland coastline and 2094 km of island territory coastline (the Andaman Islands, Nicobar Islands and Lakshadweep). Nine states and two union territories[j] have access to the sea; however, despite the huge potential, there are only 13 major ports and 200 notified minor and intermediate ports. According to the Ministry of Shipping, approximately 95% and 70% of India's trade by volume and value, respectively, goes through river and sea routes.

The biggest problem in the freight industry is that the government has not been able to modernise the main ports due to pressures from unions. As a result, the ports in India are manually operated and this has a direct effect on efficiency. Political pressure, lack of independence, lack of incentives, excessive bureaucracy and hierarchical rigidity contribute to the state of the ports in India. However, despite the labour problems at ports, Wu and Lin (2008) found that the freight industry was more competitive than the rest of the transportation industry. Their Data Envelopment Analysis (DEA) analysis suggested that, among the ports examined in industrialised countries, the efficiency of the container port in India was second only to the US port of Los Angeles.

The Indian railway is the fourth largest rail network. It had an established route length of 66,687 km in 2016 and is divided into broad, metre and narrow gauges. The total planned investment during 2007–15 was approximately USD 53.85 billion.

---

[j] Nine states (Gujarat, Maharashtra, Goa, Karnataka, Kerala, Tamil Nadu, Andhra Pradesh, Odisha, West Bengal) and two union territories (Daman & Diu and Puducherry).

4 PROBLEMS WITH WATER RESOURCES

In 2002, the Coca-Cola Company was accused of devastating the liveli-hood resources of tribes, the landless Dalit and small and marginal farm-ers in Plachimada, Kerala. The Kerala Ground Water Board confirmed the depletion of groundwater. The increased economic activity in India after liberalisation has contributed towards the declining water levels. The drying of open wells has been observed throughout India and, along with pumping and the utilisation of water by industry, has caused prolonged droughts. This is a classic case of clashing interests between forces of economic develop-ment, social marginalisation and environmental concerns.

Table 1.6 shows that India is not generally considered to be a water-deficit country. The problem is mostly related to the distribution of water between the various stakeholders. The question is how to decide who gets to utilise the water resources and how? India has historically never relied on the pricing of water as a resource, and local communities did not pay to access water for agricultural or household use; however, a problem develops when a large external consumer moves in and competes for these resources.

From the perspective of positive economics, one must look at the costs and benefits that pollution (i.e. groundwater depletion) imposes on society. If Coca-Cola depletes water, the costs include sustaining any livelihoods (i.e. farming and fishing) that are water dependent, whereas the benefits include any employment, profit and income generated by the company. It

Table 1.6 Overview of water resources of India

Water resource at a glance	Quantity (Millimetres)	%
Annual precipitation (including snowfall)	4,000	100
Precipitation during monsoon season	3,000	75
Evaporation and soil water	2,131	53.3
Average annual potential flow in rivers	1,869	46.7
Estimated utilisable water resources	1,123	28.1
Surface water	690	17.3
Replenishable groundwater	433	10.8
Storage created from utilisable water	253.381	22.52
Storage (under construction) of utilisable water	50.737	4.5

is important to note that part of this corporate income is also passed on to the government in the form of tax. If the gains outweigh the costs, then pollution is good for society.

Going back to the Coca-Cola example, one can think of a number of solutions to tackle the problem of pollution: (1) tell Coca-Cola to reduce production, (2) build canals for the residents living in near the plant to supplement the lost groundwater, and (3) relocate all residents in the neighbourhood and using the land solely for producing Coca-Cola.

In this scenario, interest groups apparently suggested the third option; however, would this really be the optimum solution? True, there would be lower groundwater depletion. However, society would lose if the cost of the factory shutting exceeded the cost of building a new canal to bring water to the region. This is also true for the third option, if the cost of relocation was less than the loss from shutting the Coca-Cola plant, then the efficiency lies in relocating those living in the neighbourhood rather than closing the factory. This idea was first propounded by Ronald Coase and is known as Coase Theorem in economics; however, Coase Theorem has some limitations related to transaction costs and the free-rider problem. If anyone in the neighbourhood wants compensation from Coca-Cola, they must negotiate with the company or with the government to build supply-side infrastructure in the form of a canal. The negotiation will cost that person both time and money; however, if they are successful all the neighbourhood will benefit. Therefore no one in the neighbourhood wants to be the negotiator, and this is the free-rider problem.

The government can help here; however, people should be more eager to inhabit a less-polluted environment. Although developed nations consume more fossil fuel, their major cities enjoy a much cleaner environment than in India. In the United States, all factories are located on the outskirts of cities. American consumers are willing to pay higher prices (in the form of taxes) for having clean cities, and hence the US government has no problems implementing a strict environmental policy.

In addition to the market solution, the GOI envisaged the idea of interlinking the major perennial rivers from the north of India to the seasonal rivers in the south of India through its nodal National Water Development Agency. In theory, a river-linking project will not only prevent the colossal water wastage by mitigating against flood and detaining flowing surface water and the erosion of topsoil during rainy seasons but will also ensure availability of water to drier areas, thus simultaneously combating both flood and drought.

Two major projects have been undertaken: the first linking the Godavari and Krishna rivers in Andhra Pradesh and the second project linking the Ken and Betwa rivers in Madhya Pradesh and Uttar Pradesh, respectively. The projects were completed in September 2016 and December 2016, respectively. The GOI has projected that the water need in 2050 will be approximately 1450 km^3, which will amount to a deficit of 327 km^3. The interlinking projects will provide an additional 200 km^3 of water, thus reducing the estimated deficit to 127 km^3. The project is expected to create around 87 million acres of irrigated land and will generate 34,000 MW of hydropower; however, half a million people are likely to be displaced in the process. Therefore although the USD 168 billion projects to interlink rivers is finally underway, it will still not be sufficient to alleviate the deficit and will create internal displacement. Several geoscientists and environmentalists have warned that the project is imprudent and dangerous, especially since there is little clarity on the ultimate impact of such a massive undertaking.

4.1 PPPs and the Financial Sector

It is generally accepted that PPPs are a useful and essential mode of infrastructure and public service delivery. Although PPPs are not a universal solution to structural problems in governance and public goods, governments are using them to develop a quantum of their country's infrastructure. In the context of this objective, governments provide substantive roles for one of the PPPs to provide clear services as a means of investing the private sector in the operational efficiency and supply of public goods.

India has witnessed considerable growth in PPPs in the last 15 years, increasing the outlay from USD 629 million to USD 16,363 million. India has emerged as one of the leading PPP markets in the world due to several policies and institutional initiatives taken by the central and state governments.

In 1990–92, there were three projects by Reliance ADA Group, Infrastructure Leasing & Financial Services of India and Synergic Resources Corporation of United States of America. During 2014–16 the top three sponsors were

The growing PPP trends, especially over the last 20 years (Table 1.7), justify the need for an elaborated policy framework that defines the principles for implementing a larger number of projects in different sectors to complement the inclusive growth spectrum of the nation. The national PPP policy seeks to facilitate this expansion in the use of the PPP approach, where necessary, in a consistent and effective manner. As a result, the GOI has set up a website dedicated to the PPP infrastructure projects to provide PPP structural toolkits (Table 1.8).

Table 1.7 Growth of investment in PPP in India

| Sector | Investment in projects by sector (USD million) | |
	1990–92	2014–16
Electricity	627	5,895
Ports	0	1,103
Railways	0	80
Roads	2	5,705
Water and sewerage	0	19

PPP, Private public partnership.
Source: www.worldbank.org

Table 1.8 Top 10 sponsors of PPP during 2014–16

Project	Country	Investment (USD million)
Reliance Communications Limited	India	29,001
Bharti Airtel Limited	India	23,879
Vodafone Essar	India	17,053
Idea Cellular	India	11,284
Tata Teleservices Limited	India	7,538
NTPC Limited	India	5,992
Shyam Telelink Ltd.	India	5,313
Mundra Ultra Mega Power Plant	India	4,200
Sasan Ultra Mega Power Plant	India	3,986
Jindal Tamnar Power Plant Phase I and II	India	3,983

The GOI endeavoured to build an enabling legal frame and financial work in the road sector. GOI has accorded the status of an industry via Section 18 (1) (12) of the Infrastructure Act. The GOI initially permitted automatic approval for foreign equity participation of up to 74% for construction and the maintenance of highways, roads and tunnels. Foreign equity participation up to 100%, subject to a ceiling of USD 300 million, was permitted following a subsequent revision. Although the GOI has been clear about the financial requirements of the PPP model, it has been hampered by a lack of financial deepening of the economy.

For the financial sector, one of the peculiarities of India's macroeconomic development has been the disproportionate weight of physical savings. Even as the aggregate savings rate reached 37% in 2008, nearly 40% of this was savings in physical assets. The financial savings of the household sector account for approximately 8% of the GDP. While a low level of financial savings reflects a lack of deepening of financial markets, its coexistence with high aggregate savings reflects the lack of a formal link between physical assets and financial markets. The two have operated in isolation not only as investment classes but across income categories and investor types.

It is in this context that the move by the Securities and Exchange Board of India to establish the Real Estate Investment Trusts (REITs) must be seen. A REIT is a listed entity that owns and manages a portfolio of income-generating real estate assets across sectors. The establishment of REITs, for which the global market is approximately USD 850 billion, will go a long way to restoring the balance between savings in physical and financial assets.

In the case of coal, which India has in abandon, mining is hampered by monopolistic Coal India, which cannot mine coal fast enough for the growing economy. The demand for coal is increasing at a much higher rate (around 8.5%) than growth in the Indian economy (around 6.5%). The spillover of these shortages has resulted in significant electricity shortages in India that pose a grave threat to the country's economic growth. Given the inefficiency of the sector, the GOI plans to raise coal output in the country by introducing a PPP model in the sector. Private and foreign mining companies say that they would participate in the coal mining projects if the government provides them with more ownership rights. These mining companies are waiting to see if the PPP model offers more than just a mine developer-cum-operator (MDO) role. According to the MDO model that is currently in use at Coal India, private parties are just contractors that are paid a fixed fee for every tonne of coal mined (http://www.powertoday. in/). The most critical deficit facing the economy is the natural resource deficit. Besides importing two-thirds of its oil requirement, India is projected to overtake China as the world's largest coal importer in the next decade, even though China's coal consumption is currently six-fold higher than that of India.

Table 1.3 shows that only three port projects were under consideration during 2014–16, with an investment of USD 1103 million. Although this is a significant increase from 1990 to 1992, the opportunity and potential for the expansion of coastal connectivity is enormous. The GOI has realised this potential and introduced financial initiatives under Section 80 IA, where investors are offered a 100% rebate on income tax for 10 consecutive years in the first 20 years of a port-related project. Guidelines were issued by the GOI to enable major ports to establish joint ventures with foreign ports, minor ports and private companies. These guidelines also encouraged state governments to provide initiatives for minor ports.

Indian Railways (IR) undertook USD 80 million worth of PPP projects during 2014–16 (Table 1.7). Over the years the IR has gone through various PPP projects including laying new lines, doubling the existing lines, enhancing port connectivity and electrifying its network. India's first 'private' railway station, Habibganj, has recently been developed near Bhopal under a PPP model where the private firm was given a concession to develop vacant lands near the Habibganj station. For the purpose of using vacant railway land, IR completed most of the work related to the digitisation of the land record (i.e. details of the acquisition, area, usage and land plans) using the Land Management Module. This also helped IR to keep digitised details of vacant plots of land measuring more than 1 acre and to chalk out the blueprint for monetisation of its vacant land in the same spirit of private development at Habibganj station.

5 CONCLUSION

Land and water are two important resources that are essential for economic development. Although India's economy is fast growing, it ranks lowly among other similar economies in in terms of its developmental indicators. Reasons for this may be a lack of both physical and social infrastructure. This chapter has demonstrated how land and water are important resources, yet how they are frequently misused. This has important repercussions not only on more uniform development but also on the distribution of income. Lack of transparency in the allocation of land and crony capitalism may lead to an inefficient use of resources. The Supreme Court of India has recently become cognizant of these facts and implemented stringent laws to prevent the misuse of land and water resources.

REFERENCES

Bardhan, P., 2011. Land Acquisition: Currently a Major Stumbling Block for Development Policy. Development Outreach, World Bank.

Ghatak, M., Ghosh, P., 2011. The land acquisition bill: a critique and a proposal. Econ. Polit. Weekly 46 (41), 65–72.

Singh, R., 2012. Inefficiency and abuse of compulsory land acquisition: an enquiry into the way forward. Centre for Development Economics, Working Paper No. 209, Delhi School of Economics, Delhi.

Wu, Y.J., Lin, C., 2008. National port competitiveness: implications for India. Manag. Decis. 46 (10), 1482–1507.

FURTHER READINGS

Sarma, E.A., 2015. Lack of clarity and vision in the new mines and minerals act. Econ. Polit. Weekly 50 (15).

Singh, R., 2010. Delays and cost overruns in infrastructure projects: extent, causes and remedies. Econ. Polit. Weekly XLV (21).

Singh, L.B., Kalidindi, S.N., 2006. Traffic revenue risk management through Annuity Model of PPP road projects in India. Int. J. Proj. Manag. 24 (7), 605–613.

CHAPTER 2

India's Exports Through the Lens of Diversification

Seema Sangita
TERI School of Advanced Studies, New Delhi, India

1 INTRODUCTION

Amidst a slowdown in the global economy, India's export growth remained robust during 2012–15; however, recent data regarding India's exports are a matter of concern. This chapter aims to study the trends in exports of India between 1996 and 2016, with a particular focus on the phase after the start of global recession in 2008–09. Diversification of trading partners and commodity baskets have been suggested as strategies to help developing- and emerging-market economies cope with recessions. Therefore this chapter also investigates if India has diversified its partners, and a similar analysis was carried out with respect to diversification of commodity baskets at the HS2 and an HS6 level. A greater concentration of commodity baskets was found, which may indicate higher exposure to risk in global markets. There was also some evidence that India diversified its export markets and that this could have contributed towards sustained export growth.

The World Economic Outlook Report, which was published by the IMF in October 2016, stated that 'the decline in real trade growth has been broad-based. Few countries were spared the 2012–15 slowdown in trade growth, either in absolute terms or relative to GDP growth' (IMF, 2016b). However, it appears that India is one of the few countries that escaped an immediate slowdown in its exports after the global recession. While the world was trying to cope with a recession, India's exports grew at double-digit rates in 2010–11. The growth in exports persisted until the sudden collapse in 2015–16.

It is postulated that the diversification of trade, which involves creating a diversified set of trading partners and a diversified commodity basket, is a critical strategy for a country to survive against the risks posed by globalised markets. This chapter attempts to study the trends of trading partner diversity and industry-commodity diversity in Indian exports. Apart from analysing the trends of different export indicators, this paper also employs

Changing the Indian Economy
http://dx.doi.org/10.1016/B978-0-08-102005-0.00002-2

a Herfindahl–Hirschman Index (HHI) of export diversity to explore if any increase in export diversity occurred between 1996 and 2006. The selected time frame represents an interesting phase in India's export growth. For example, export growth was relatively tepid until 2000, after which it rapidly increased. In terms of constant 2010 USD, India's export tripled from 2000 to 2007. The global financial crisis in 2009 was merely a minor hiccup as this rapid export growth continued until 2014; however, this was subsequently followed by a downturn in exports. This chapter attempts to understand the links between these export trends and diversification of importers and commodity baskets.

The recent stagnation and downturn in Indian exports are of concern. Several studies advocated diversity as one method for improving productivity; for example, UNCTAD (2013) predicted a slowdown in Indian exports and emphasised the need to improve the export diversity by identifying new markets and new products. Das Krishna and Kumar (2015) also identified a decline in exports across all sectors from December 2014 and reported that India 'has failed to claim a large market share in any export product category in the world. It does not have depth in any export product or any market'. A Ministry of Finance, Government of India Report also expressed concern over the slow growth of Indian exports and identified export diversification as the main strategy to overcome the slowdown in exports (Prasad, 2017). However, none of these papers measured trade diversity to develop an understanding of the existing diversity in commodity basket and trading partners and suggested a strategy for the future on this basis. This chapter attempts to address this oversight by calculating and analysing the HHI over the last 2 decades.

There appears to be a concomitant increase in the diversification of trading partners and export growth. It seems likely that the growth in the diversity of trading partners during the pre-crisis stage helped to mitigate the effects of the recession. Conversely, in terms of industry and commodities, there appears to be an increase in the concentration of exports rather than the diversity. One sector where this concentration occurred was the oil and petroleum sector. The rationale behind diversifying the commodity basket is to mitigate the risk of idiosyncratic events in any one market. India's export basket was dominated by the oil and petroleum sector and hence it was not easy to mitigate the impact of a 75% collapse in the crude oil prices after 2014.

Section 2 of this chapter explores the trends in India's exports over the last 2 decades. The concept of diversity is explored in Section 3, followed by an analysis of Indian exports with respect to trading partner diversity and commodity basket diversity in Sections 4 and 5. Finally, Section 6 presents some concluding remarks.

2 INDIA'S EXPORTS OVER THE LAST 2 DECADES

India's exports increased more than five-fold over the 2 decades from 1996 to 2016 when measured in constant 2010 USD; however, it is surprising that a large part of this growth occurred between 2009 and 2013 when the rest of the world was reeling from a severe economic downturn. This phase followed a previous spell of high export growth from 2002 to 2008, which was in tandem with buoyant global economies.

However, the more recent growth phase in the Indian export market tells a very different story. Global trade dipped in 2009 and has remained sluggish since. The world trade volumes and global industrial production stagnated, and one consequence of the downturn was the destruction of demand from richer economies (Gangnes et al., 2015; IMF, 2016a,b). However, India's exporting sector demonstrated impressive resilience against this recession. As demonstrated in Table 2.1, the immediate impact of the recession was seen by a negative growth rate in exports in 2009. However, in 2010 and 2011, the growth rate in exports was approximately 20% and 15%, respectively. Even if some of this growth was attributed to a low base effect, the magnitude of the increase in the value of exports remains substantial. Although the growth rate was not as dramatic in the subsequent years, it did remain relatively high; however, a slowdown was observed from 2014 onwards.

India's exports as a ratio of world trade rose consistently over the last decade, even through the post-2009 turmoil. Although this indicator has

Table 2.1 Growth rate of exports in India during the global recession

Year	Growth rate of exports
2008	14.60
2009	−4.69
2010	19.62
2011	15.58
2012	6.81
2013	7.79
2014	1.78
2015	−5.31
2016	4.51

Source: Author's calculation using the information presented in Fig. 2.1.

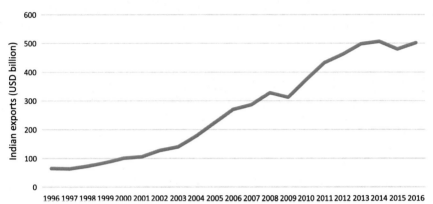

Figure 2.1 *India's exports in USD billion (constant 2010 USD).* Source: *World Bank World Development Indicators.*

increased four-fold since 1996, its magnitude remains low. Despite India's emerging market economy being relatively resilient, it has experienced limited integration with global trade. Furthermore, it also began to show signs of decline in 2015 and 2016. In contrast, India's exports as a share of GDP is substantial and has more than doubled from 10% in 1996 to 24% in 2008. This indicator declined to 20% in 2009, then rose again until 2014, but has been on a declining path ever since (see Fig. 2.2).

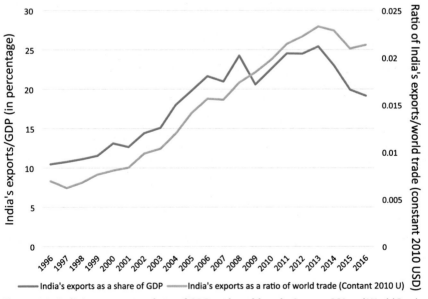

Figure 2.2 *India's exports as a share of GDP and world trade.* Source: *RBI and World Bank.*

It is possible that the analysis of gross exports from India may provide a misleading picture. Most countries, including India, operate as part of global value chains (GVCs). Gangnes et al. (2015) highlighted the importance of GVC production arrangements and showed that 'the share of GVC trade in total trade grew by more than 10% points from 40% in 1995 to 52% in 2008, before declining slightly in 2009'. In this context, gross exports may constitute a substantial amount of foreign intermediate inputs. Hence it is imperative to examine the domestic value added of exports. India's domestic value added of exports increased consistently from USD 51 billion to USD 347 billion between 2000 and 2011. In 2008, the domestic value added of Indian exports was USD 235 billion. This value fell marginally in the following year but rose to USD 300.5 billion in 2010. In conclusion, the export growth in India is a reasonably fair reflection of the value added in the country, however, this information is not available for recent years, and it is not possible to comment on whether there has been a decline in domestic value added in the last few years.[a]

3 DIVERSIFICATION AND TRADE

Diversification of trading partners and the export commodity basket is touted as a strategy that can help to alleviate the impact of recessions in different parts of the world. The rationale behind this is that the trade links between nations are deepening as part of the GVC phenomenon. Hence in circumstances where a country is not very diversified, or in other words has a few specialised commodities that are traded in selected markets, any disruption to the specific commodity market or a recession in the economy of the trading partner would substantially affect the exports. This risk may take the form of fluctuations in the exchange rate of certain currencies, inflationary conditions in certain economies or a potential of contagion when a significant volume of trade exists with vulnerable nations. Diversification of both trading partners and the commodity basket can help to mitigate these risks.

This idea is a remarkable departure from the Ricardian Theory of Comparative Advantage, which was premised on the principle that there might be gains from trade as a result of specialisation. Krugman (1980) developed the idea of product differentiation and a love for a varied approach in the

[a] Using OECD statistics, 2011 is the latest year for which this information is available.

International Trade Theory. This was based on monopolistic competition markets, where different firms in different markets may produce and trade different varieties of the same product (Ardelean, 2006; Feenstra, 2015).

Hesse (2008) presented strong evidence suggesting that export concentration is potentially harmful to economic growth and development. This paper found an inverse relationship between per-capita income and the HHI in developing countries (i.e. Malaysia, Thailand, Chile and Uganda) between 1962 and 2000. Camanho da Costa Neto and Romeu (2011) attempted to study whether export diversification, in the context of product, industry and trade partner diversification, helped Latin American countries cope with the global financial crisis. They found that both product and industry diversification, but not trade partner diversification, supported the resilience of Latin American economies in a crisis. However, Önder and Yilmazkuday (2014) demonstrated contrasting evidence with respect to trade partner diversification. They measure trade partner diversification to understand its implications on economic growth and found that, after controlling for a wide variety of growth-influencing factors, trade with a diverse set of partners positively influences growth.

One approach to measuring diversity is the HHI. HHI is a traditional method for measuring market concentration; however, it can also be re-purposed to measure export diversification. Hence this index essentially measures the inequality between the shares of exports. These shares can be defined in different ways; however, in this chapter the focus is on the share of exports with a specific trading partner and the share of exports in a particular industry or commodity, as defined by the HS2 and HS6 codes in the classification of goods (Cadot et al., 2013; Camanho da Costa Neto and Romeu, 2011).

The HHI is defined as: subscript n in equation

$$HHI = \sum_{n=1}^{N} s_n^2$$

A lower value of the HHI indicates a higher export diversification and vice versa. In this chapter, HHI is calculated for three cases:

1. where n indicates the trading partner, N indicates the total number of trading partners and s_n is the share of value of exports that goes to the nth trading partner,
2. where n indicates the industry as measured by the two-digit HS codes, N indicates the total number of industries and s_n is the share of value of exports of the nth industry,

3. where n indicates the commodity as measured by the six–digit HS codes, N indicates the total number of commodities exported by India and s_n is the share of value of exports of the nth commodity.

For this analysis, India's export data were used at a bilateral level and at a commodity level provided by the Ministry of Commerce, DGCIS, Kolkata and the Government of India. The HHI was calculated between 1996–97 and 2016–17. The dataset indicated that India had approximately 220–240 trading partners during this time frame. Indian exports covered all industry categories at the HS2 digit level and approximately 4500–5500 commodity categories at the HS6 digit level in this time frame.

4 INDIA'S EXPORTS AND ITS TRADING PARTNERS

Table 2.2 reports the top importers from India between 1996–97 and 2016–17. This section also looks closely at two time periods following the global financial crisis, namely, 2009–10 and 2013–14.

One indication of limited diversification of trading partners is that the United States is consistently the largest importer from India, except in the aftermath of the crisis in 2009–10. Interestingly, the value of exports from India to the United States continued to rise, and between 1996–97 and 2016–17 had risen from USD 6.56 billion to USD 42.33 billion. The value of exports more than doubled between 2006–07 and 2013–14 despite the global financial crisis. The United Arab Emirates has emerged as the second largest importer from India, and the value of exports has grown from USD 1.5 billion to over USD 30 billion.

However, a different picture emerges when the data are inspected more closely. In 1996–97, Bangladesh was the only developing or emerging market economy to feature in the top 10 importers from India. Japan was an important trading partner in the 1990s, and Hong Kong and Singapore have consistently traded with India over this time. However, in subsequent years, China has gained prominence as a trading partner. Other countries from mainland Europe (i.e. Germany, Belgium and Italy) were important importers from India before the financial crisis. By 2016–17, Vietnam and Bangladesh were among India's top trading partners, thus indicating a switch away from mainland Europe towards Asian nations. This diversification of trading partners potentially reflects the response of western countries to the sluggish growth after the financial crisis.

The HHI provides a broader picture of the diversification of trading partners over time. The results of the HHI calculation for trading partners

Table 2.2 Top Indian export markets (USD billion)

	1996–97		2006–07		2009–10		2013–14		2016–17
Importer	Value of exports	Importer	Value of exports	Importer	Value of exports	Importer	Value of exports	Importer	Value of exports
United States	6.56	United States	18.86	United Arab Emirates	23.97	United States	39.14	United States	42.33
UK	2.05	United Arab Emirates	12.02	United States	19.54	United Arab Emirates	30.52	United Arab Emirates	31.31
Japan	2.01	China P RP	8.32	China P RP	11.62	China P RP	14.82	Hong Kong	14.16
Germany	1.89	Singapore	6.05	Hong Kong	7.89	Hong Kong	12.73	China P RP	10.20
Hong Kong	1.86	UK	5.62	Singapore	7.59	Singapore	12.51	Singapore	9.57
United Arab Emirates	1.48	Hong Kong	4.69	Netherlands	6.40	Saudi Arabia	12.22	UK	8.56
Belgium	1.09	Germany	3.98	UK	6.22	UK	9.78	Germany	7.21
Singapore	0.98	Italy	3.58	Germany	5.41	Netherlands	8.00	Vietnam Soc Rep	6.82
Italy	0.93	Belgium	3.48	Saudi Arabia	3.91	Germany	7.52	Bangladesh P R	6.73
Bangladesh P R	0.87	Japan	2.87	France	3.82	Japan	6.81	Belgium	5.67

2016–17 pertains to the financial year from April 2016 to March 2017.
Source: DGCIS and Ministry of Commerce.

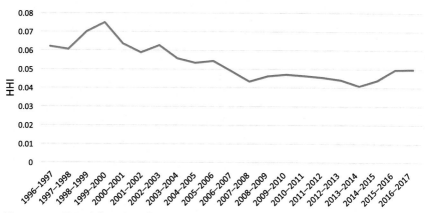

Figure 2.3 *HHI of diversity of trading partners.* Source: *Author's calculation using data from the DGCIS and Ministry of Commerce.*

is presented in Fig. 2.3. The HHI ranges from roughly 0.04 to 0.075. The magnitude of this number is rather small as a large number of trading partners are being considered in this study. Hence it is more instructive to focus on the direction of HHI change. An increasing trend was observed in the HHI until the year 2000 when the HHI adopted a predominantly declining trend, with minor fluctuations until 2013–14. A falling HHI indicates a lower concentration or a greater diversification of trading partners, thus indicating that the export growth before the crisis was concomitant with a rise in the diversification of trading partners. In the phase following the crisis, HHI fell from 0.047 to 0.04 between 2009–10 and 2013–14. Finally, it rose as the exports fell during the last 3 years of the study. This clearly indicates an alignment between the diversification of trading partners and export growth in India. The correlation coefficient between HHI and exports (measured in constant 2010 USD) was −0.84. While it is premature to draw any inferences regarding the direction of causality, this certainly establishes a link between export growth and the diversity of trading partners. The improvement in the diversity of partners from 2000 to 2007 possibly enabled the sustained growth of exports during and immediately after the crisis. It is possible that some trading partners stopped importing from India as a direct result of the crisis, which may be reflected in the stagnant HHI, but the diversification that took place prior to this may have helped to absorb the loss and enable export growth in the gloomy global economic scenario. Improving the diversity of trading partners with proactive bilateral and multilateral trade agreements could possibly help to increase exports in India.

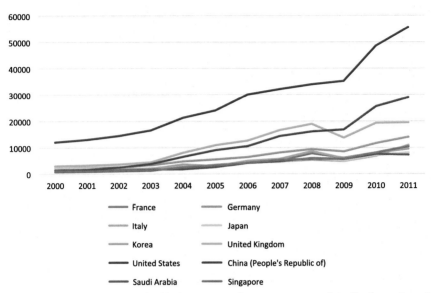

Figure 2.4 *Domestic value-added content of gross exports of India for selected importers.* Source: *From OECD (2016), Trade in Value Added Database, http://stats.oecd. org/index.aspx?DatasetCode=TIVA_2016_C1 (Data extracted on 16 Jul 2017).*

The increase in bilateral trade is not merely at the level of gross exports. Fig. 2.4 illustrates the domestic value-added content of gross exports from India with a few trading partners (i.e. the United States, China, the UK and Germany). Overall, there was a rising trend in the domestic value added at the bilateral level with these trading partners. The magnitude and the growth of domestic value-added content of exports was highest in the United States between 2000 and 2011. Interestingly, there was a higher rate of growth after the 2009 financial crash. The second and third largest importers in terms of the domestic value-added content of exports were China and the UK. China demonstrated continual growth with a trend similar to that of the United States; however, for the UK, there was some evidence of a fall and stagnation of the domestic value-added content of exports after the crisis. The magnitude of the domestic value-added content of exports was generally lower for most other bilateral trading partners, but the values all increased between 2000 and 2011.

5 DIVERSITY OF THE COMMODITY BASKET

The top exporting industries in India are reported in Table 2.3. Gems and jewellery have been two of the largest exporting sectors in India over the 2 decades from the mid-1990s to 2016–17. The value of exports in these sectors has consistently increased from USD 4.77 billion to USD 43.78 billion. However,

Table 2.3 Top exporting industries at the HS2 level (in USD billion)

1996–97		2006–07		2009–10		2013–14		2016–17	
HS code	Exports	HS code	Exports	HS code	Exports	HS code	Exports	HS code	Exports
71	4.77	27	18.86	71	29.20	27	64.69	71	43.78
52	2.83	71	16.09	27	29.04	71	41.69	27	32.28
62	2.72	29	5.74	29	7.45	87	12.93	87	15.02
03	1.12	72	5.60	85	7.23	84	12.08	84	14.14
10	1.10	62	5.29	84	7.19	29	12.02	30	12.97
84	1.05	84	5.10	26	6.65	30	11.14	29	11.74
61	1.03	26	4.90	87	6.17	10	10.56	62	9.21
23	1.00	85	4.11	62	6.13	85	10.30	72	8.73
29	0.99	52	3.94	99	5.20	52	9.93	61	8.27
87	0.90	87	3.77	30	5.19	72	9.22	85	8.24

HS code definitions

03	Fish and crustaceans, molluscs and other aquatic invertebrates
10	Cereals
23	Residues and waste from the food industries and prepared animal fodder
26	Ores, slag and ash
27	Mineral fuels, mineral oils and products of their distillation; bituminous substances; mineral waxes
29	Organic chemicals
30	Pharmaceutical products
52	Cotton
61	Articles of apparel and clothing accessories, knitted or crocheted
62	Articles of apparel and clothing accessories, not knitted or crocheted
71	Natural or cultured pearls, precious or semiprecious stones, premetals clad with premetal and articles thereof, imitation jewellery and coins
72	Iron and steel
84	Nuclear reactors, boilers, machinery, mechanical appliances and parts thereof
85	Electrical machinery and equipment and parts thereof, sound recorders and reproducers, television image and sound recorders and reproducers and parts thereof
87	Vehicles other than railway or tramway rolling stock and parts and accessories thereof
99	Miscellaneous goods

the oil and petroleum sector dominated the export scene in the post-crisis time frame. This sector did not feature among the top 10 exporting industries in India in 1996–97 but featured on the top of the list in the following decade. In terms of the value of exports, there is a huge difference between the top two industries and all other industries. This indicates a higher concentration of these two industries in the exporting sector. This difference was particularly stark in 2009–10, when exports from the top two sectors (i.e. gems and jewellery and oil and petroleum) were close to USD 29 billion each. The third highest export industry is the organic chemicals industry, which accounts for a mere USD 7 billion. This indicates that Indian exports sustained the country through the economic crisis, particularly through the oil and petroleum sector. However, this level of concentration is risky, and the growth of exports would depend heavily on global prices in a sector that has experienced volatility in the recent past. In 2016–17, oil and petroleum exports remained the top exporting sector; however, there was a drastic decline in the value of exports from USD 64.7 billion to USD 43.8 billion.

India appeared to move away from agricultural and allied exports of industries such as cereals and fish in favour of sectors such as electrical machinery during the 2000s. However, in the post-crisis phase, raw cotton and cereals were occasionally within the top 10 exporting sectors. The export of ores also increased during 2006–07 and 2009–10. These commodities tend to be at the lower end of the value chain and are also heavily dependent on global prices. Exports from the iron and steel industry picked up in the post-crisis era. HS codes 84, 85 and 87 represent industries that are higher up in the value chain (i.e. vehicles, mechanical and electric appliances and equipment and machinery), and these industries became more important exporting sectors after the global crisis.

Another industry that is gaining importance in the export basket of India is the pharmaceutical sector. This sector had the tenth largest value of exports in 2009–10 and improved its ranking to fifth by 2016–17.

The HHI indices for the two-digit HS code industries and the six-digit commodities are presented in Fig. 2.5. Given the greater number of

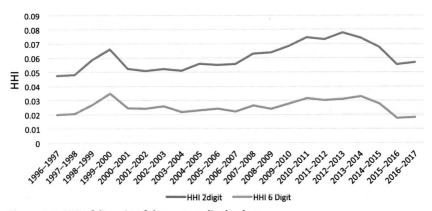

Figure 2.5 *HHI of diversity of the commodity basket.*

commodities than industries, the HHI of commodities is lower. However, in terms of trends, both indices run almost parallel to each other. The HHI increased sharply during the 3 years from 1997–2000, but after that, the decline in HHI was just as steep. However, a steady increase in the HHI was observed during the 2000s, indicating a concentration of exports at the two-digit level until 2012–13. At the same time, the HHI of the six-digit HS code stagnated with a marginal increase after 2009–10. There was a fall in the HHI of both industries and commodities after 2013.

Overall, it appears as if specialisation or concentration rather than diversification of the commodity basket influences export growth. Although this may support high rates of growth, the risk exposure is also significantly higher. This information may be insufficient to draw any conclusions on causation; however, the correlation coefficient of exports in India (measured in constant 2010 USD) and the HHI the two-digit and a six-digit level was 0.67 and 0.15. This indicates a positive correlation between specialisation and export growth, and this effect is stronger at a sectoral level than at a commodity level.

In contrast to the HHI of trading partners, there is evidence of an increase in the concentration of industries and commodities. This supports the aforementioned evidence regarding the dominance of two sectors (i.e. gems and jewellery and oil and petroleum) in the export market. The fall in the HHI in the last few years could reflect a collapse in the markets of these dominating sectors. The Brent crude oil prices dropped by nearly 75% from 102.63 on 31 January 2013 to 29.78 on the same day in 2016. Average crude oil import costs (USD per barrel) showed a steady decline from 2011 to 2016 (Table 2.4). This explains the drastic drop in the export value of oil

Table 2.4 Average crude oil import costs

Year	Average crude oil import costs (USD/barrel)
2008	94.97
2009	58.83
2010	76.02
2011	102.43
2012	101.16
2013	97.25
2014	89.43
2015	45.83
2016	37.94

Volume-weighted average costs for France, Germany, Italy, Spain, the UK, Japan, Canada and the United States.
Source: Based on IEA data from Crude oil import prices © OECD/IEA, 2018 doi: 10.1787/9ee0e3ab-en.

and petroleum, and consequently explains the slowdown of the aggregate exports in India. This reflects the realisation of the risks of concentrating all exports in one sector. It is possible that the recent collapse in the value of exports could have been avoided by appropriate diversification of the export basket.

6 CONCLUSION

At a time when global trade was slowing down, India's exports were doing surprisingly well. However, this story took a turn for the worse after 2014 which marks the beginning of a consistent decline of the value of Indian exports.

Developing and emerging market countries have been encouraged to hedge the risks of exchange rates, other price volatilities and contagion through diversification. This diversification can occur across two axes: trading partners and the commodity basket. This chapter investigates the role of diversified trading partners and commodity baskets in India's story of sustained growth in the aftermath of the global financial crisis.

This research found that India consistently increased its diversity of trading partners and that this may have helped sustain the growth of its exports. At the same time, there is evidence of specialisation of commodities rather than diversification. It is possible that this helped to retain the high level of export growths but with a higher risk from a more concentrated commodity basket. This risk may have started to show an effect, as the decline of exports in 2016–17 could well be attributed to the issues in the global oil markets.

Interestingly, this result is in contrast to the evidence provided by Camanho da Costa Neto and Romeu (2011) who found that diversification of trading partners had little effect compared to the concentration of the commodity basket in the resilience of exports from Latin American companies after the global financial crisis.

Given the limitations of the data, few concrete inferences can be drawn on the nature and direction of causality; however, this study established a need to further explore the implications of diversified trading partners and commodities. There are strong policy implications that could be used to design and implement bilateral and multilateral trading agreements to diversify trading partners. The task of diversifying the commodity basket is equally important and will require major structural changes in the Indian economy, improved infrastructure, upgrading of technology and appropriate capital investment to revive existing and create new export-oriented industries. Government policies should also aim to integrate India into a range of diverse GVCs.

REFERENCES

Ardelean, A., 2006. How strong is the love of variety? Purdue CIBER Working Papers. Paper 46. Available from: http://docs.lib.purdue.edu/ciberwp/46.

Cadot, O., Carrère, C., Strauss-Kahn, V., 2013. Trade diversification, income, and growth: what do we know? J. Econ. Surv. 27, 790–812. doi: 10.1111/j.1467-6419.2011.00719.x.

Camanho da Costa Neto, N., Romeu, R., 2011. Did export diversification soften the impact of the global financial crisis? IMF Working paper WP/11/99.

Das Krishna, G., Kumar, R., 2015. Indian exports loss of global competitiveness. Econ. Polit. Wkly. 50 (34), 20–23, Available from: http://www.cprindia.org/sites/default/files/articles/Indian_Exports.pdf.

Feenstra, R., 2015. Advanced International Trade: Theory and Evidence Second Edition, second ed. Princeton University Press, Princeton.

Gangnes, B., Ma, A., Van Assche, A., 2015. Global value chains and the trade-income relationship: implications for the recent trade slowdown. The Global Trade Slowdown: A New Normal?. CEPR, London, Available from: http://voxeu.org/sites/default/files/file/Global%20Trade%20Slowdown_nocover.pdf.

Hesse, H., 2008. Export diversification and economic growth Growth Commission Working Paper #21. Available from: http://siteresources.worldbank.org/EXTPREMNET/Resources/489960-1338997241035/Growth_Commission_Working_Paper_21_Export_Diversification_Economic_Growth.pdf.

IMF, 2016a. World Economic Outlook: Too Slow for Too Long. IMF, Washington.

IMF, 2016b. World Economic Outlook: Subdued Demand: Symptoms and Remedies. IMF, Washington.

International Energy Agency. 2017. Monthly Oil Price Statistics – July 2017. Available from: https://www.iea.org/media/statistics/surveys/prices/mps.pdf.

Krugman, P.R., 1980. Scale economies, product differentiation, and the pattern of trade. Am. Econ. Rev. 70 (5), 950–959.

Önder, A., Yilmazkuday, H. 2014. Trade partner diversification and growth: how trade links matter. Federal Reserve Bank of Dallas, Globalization and Monetary Policy Institute Working Paper No. 192. Available from: http://www.dallasfed.org/assets/documents/institute/wpapers/2014/0192.pdf.

Prasad, H.A.C., 2017. Reviving and accelerating India's exports: policy issues and suggestions. Ministry of Finance, Government of India, Working Paper No. 1/2017-DEA. Available from: http://dea.gov.in/sites/default/files/RevivingAcceleratingIndiaExports_Issues_Suggestions.pdf.

UNCTAD, 2013. Impact of the Global Slowdown on India's Exports and Employment. UNCTAD, Geneva, Available from http://unctad.org/en/PublicationsLibrary/webditctncd2009d1_en.pdf.

CHAPTER 3

The Multiplier Effect of Developmental and Non-developmental Expenditure in India

Abhishek Kumar*, William Joe**
*Research Scholar, Central University of Gujarat, Gujarat, India
**Institute of Economic Growth, Delhi, India

1 INTRODUCTION

Public expenditure is necessary to address the diverse social, economic and regulatory requirements of an economy. The links between public expenditure and economic growth are well recognized (Ram, 1986; Romer, 1989, 1990a,b). Public expenditure also contributes towards economic growth and social development through multiple channels; for instance, investments in agricultural and industrial infrastructure creates backward and forward links and leads to employment opportunities. Similarly, investments in health and education can lead to higher labour productivity and contribute towards economic growth (Devarajan et al., 1996; Landau, 1986; Miller and Russek, 1997). While public expenditure is expected to generate significant growth–multiplier effects, there are several constraints when deciding upon the magnitude of public expenditure. The effectiveness of public expenditure is particularly sensitive to the composition of expenditure allocations and the state of the fiscal environment.

Public expenditure is broadly composed of both developmental and non-developmental expenditure. The former refers to expenditure incurred directly for enhancing economic and social services, whereas the latter includes expenditure for the maintenance of law and order, defence and other general activities and government services. Both types of expenditure include components of revenue and capital expenditure. Public investments in capital formation have higher growth benefits than similar levels of revenue expenditure. Although these expenditures are not necessarily substitutable, in case of India there is greater scope for substitution (Bose and Bhanumurthy, 2013). Studies have explored the effect of public expenditure on

Changing the Indian Economy
http://dx.doi.org/10.1016/B978-0-08-102005-0.00003-4

economic growth in India, but only a few have assessed the multiplier effect of developmental and non-developmental expenditure on economic growth (Bhattacharya, 1984; Jain and Kumar, 2013; Krishnamurty, 1985). The effect of developmental expenditure is expected to be positive as investments in priority areas (i.e. infrastructure and human capital formation) can provide a growth spurt. Developmental expenditure can further increase the efficiency of resources and push the economy toward higher growth trajectories. For instance, investments in transport, storage and communication infrastructure could lead to a reduction in inflation volatility by removing structural bottle-necks. Given such benefits, the timely and systematic analysis of the growth impact associated with developmental and non-developmental purposes are salient for policymaking in developing countries.

These studies were based on pre-liberalisation settings or consider the pre-liberalisation period in their estimation of the multiplier effects; however, sub-stantial changes have occurred in the fiscal environment and economic poli-cies of India post-liberalisation and these can affect the conclusions regarding multiplier effects and magnitude (Ilzetzki et al., 2013; Koh, 2017). Following the adoption of a new economic policy in the 1990s (and more recently the great financial crisis), containing fiscal deficits of the union and state govern-ments was the key target of the fiscal policy (under the Fiscal Responsibil-ity and Budget Management Act, FRBM Act, 2003). Therefore this chapter focuses on developmental and non-developmental expenditure and estimates the multiplier effects in the post-liberalisation period (1990–2013) in India. Insights regarding the effectiveness of developmental and non-developmental public expenditure can contribute toward policy debates on fiscal prudence.

The remainder of the chapter is organized as follows: Section 2 presents an overview of the economic theories regarding the growth benefits of public expenditure and reviews the evidence on multiplier effects for developed and developing countries, including India. This section also lists the econometric alternatives for robust estimation of the multiplier effects. Section 3 describes the data and methods used for the analysis. Section 4 presents the key findings obtained when using the structural vector auto-regression (SVAR) model to test the effectiveness of the specified categories of public expenditure. Section 5 concludes by discussing the policy implications and the limitations of the study.

2 REVIEW OF THE LITERATURE

The classical school of thought promoted a laissez-faire approach whereby public expenditure was confined to the maintenance of law and order and other essential government activities (i.e. defence). However, following the

Great Depression, the Keynesian Revolution established an indispensable role for public expenditure in determining the level of income and employment in an economy. The upshot of the general theory was the need for government intervention in the management of aggregate demand (Keynes, 1936). The concept of the fiscal multiplier was credited to Kahn (1931) but was popularized by Keynes (1936). Later, Hicks (1950) advanced the concept to the super-multiplier, which combined the effect of increased investment due to increased income along with the multiplier. The Keynesian approach was initially synonymous with fiscal policies but the role of monetary factors was also subsequently appreciated by the Keynesians (Tobin, 1987, 1997). However, following the 1970s stagflation, the Keynesian approach was subsided by alternative theoretical views on the limited efficacy of public spending on economic stability (Monetarism, New Classical and Real Business Cycle School). Nevertheless, New Keynesians maintained that government intervention was critical for macroeconomic stability, as capitalist economies display poor speeds of convergence towards long-run equilibrium (Snowdown and Vane, 2005). The global financial crisis has also reopened the debate on the growth effectiveness of public expenditure.

Although there are vast amounts of literature on fiscal multipliers, macroeconomists lack a consensus regarding the definitive value across economies and contexts. The value of the multiplier varies during growth and recession, and inaccurate estimation could wreak havoc on the desired outcomes (Auerbach and Gorodnichenko, 2011; Blanchard and Leigh, 2013). For instance, Ilzetzki et al. (2013) used data from 44 countries to examine the role of country characteristics and concluded that the long-run fiscal multipliers were smaller in developing countries, open economies, flexible exchange rate regimes and periods of high public debt (Perotti, 1999). Studies also showed that the multiplier was sensitive to interest rates and that fiscal policy was more effective when interest rates did not respond to the fiscal stimulus (Alumnia et al., 2010; Christiano et al., 2011; Devereux, 2010; Woodford, 2011). Barro and Redlick (2009) show that fiscal multipliers will be large when there are tight conditions in the labour market.

The study regarding the effect of public expenditure on output in India gained prominence after the global financial crisis of 2008. Policy concerns due to the global shocks have increased the focus on the development of analytical models to estimate the effect of the fiscal multiplier. India has a long history of fiscal mismanagement that is associated with high levels of financial debts and deficits. Following the adoption of the FRBM Act in 2003, the union and state governments in India committed to engage in prudent fiscal spending and eliminate revenue deficits on account of unproductive spending. Thus understanding the nature and magnitude of fiscal multipliers could be helpful for formulating a strategy to wisely allocate scarce resources. In this regard, the major conclusions based on the existing studies are summarized below.

Jain and Kumar (2013) estimated the value of the multiplier for union and state government expenditure during 1980–2011. The study found that: (1) the multiplier varied for different heads of expenditure, (2) the multiplier of capital outlay was higher both in the short and long run, (3) the revenue expenditure had a sizeable impact in the short run but the effect died over time and (4) the multiplier for state-level expenditure was higher than the centre's expenditure. Bose and Bhanumurthy (2013) also confirmed the presence of a strong multiplier effect of capital expenditure on output. They also estimated the tax multiplier to be negative and suggested that output could be increased by reducing the tax rates. Estimates notwithstanding, the role of country-specific settings (i.e. trade openness, capital mobility and exchange-rate regimes) play important roles in the determination of the multiplier (Koh, 2017). The issue is of importance in India because it is an emerging market with increasing integration into the global economy. Moreover, the high unemployment and income inequalities mean that timely assessment of the multiplier effect of developmental and non-developmental expenditure is necessary to manoeuvre the fiscal space. Developmental expenditure can provide much-needed impetus to economic development by improving infrastructure and productivity; however, the ratio of developmental expenditure, which accounted for 71% of the total revenue expenditure in the India during 1980–85, has steadily declined. Its share in total revenue expenditure reduced to 55% in 2000–05 before rising marginally to 58% during 2005–10 (State Finances Report, 2009-10).

Nevertheless, there are certain methodological concerns that could affect the magnitude of the estimates. For instance, Yadav et al. (2012) measured the effect of fiscal shocks on the Indian economy during 1997–2009 but found that approaches toward series stationarity can influence the values of multipliers. From a methodological perspective, endogeneity between changes in public expenditure and output is the main concern. In this regard, Caldara and Camps (2008) highlighted four main identification schemes that could be used in the estimation of fiscal multipliers: (1) the recursive approach (Sims, 1980), (2) the traditional SVAR analysis (Blanchard and Perotti, 2002; Perotti, 2008) (3) the sign restriction approach (Uhlig, 2005) and (4) the narrative approach (Ramey and Shapiro, 1998). In the narrative approach, exogenous variation was measured using military spending as the proxy; however, Koh (2017) argue that the economic conditions in developing countries could lead to war and make military spending endogenous. Similarly, if other fiscal shocks occur at the same time, it may be hard to disentangle them from the military spending. The popularity of the SVAR based approach has increased due to its ability to capture the dynamic relationship between endogenous variables (Blanchard and Perotti, 2002; Fatas and Mihov, 2001; Perotti, 2005). The order of the variables in the Blanchard and Perotti (2002) scheme led to variation in the value of the fiscal multiplier. Assuming that government spending was exogenous and did not react to GDP in the same quarter, they used the identification scheme in which expenditure was put before GDP. The restrictions assumed by the various approaches on the output elasticity of government expenditure and tax revenue could yield different results. In India, the existing studies have mostly relied on the Blanchard and Perotti (2002) approach. Yadav et al. (2012) used the recursive scheme and the Blanchard and Perroti scheme and obtained different results for the multiplier. Jain and Kumar (2013) also used the Blanchard and Perroti scheme with government expenditure ordered before GDP growth rate and tax revenue.

3 DATA AND METHODS

Data on macroeconomic variables were sourced from the Handbook of Statistics on the Indian Economy which has been published annually by the Reserve Bank of India (RBI) since 1998. Given the absence of quarterly data for most of the variables, except GDP, the use of annual data during 1990–2013 seemed more suitable. This is also the period over which the economy gradually moved from being closed to open. The GDP figures used in the analysis were at constant 2004–05 prices. The base of the GDP series recently shifted from 2004–05 to 2011–12. The latest official data for GDP (at 2004–05 base) is available for 2013–14. The output gap was calculated using the Hodrick–Prescott filter using $\lambda = 100$, which was deemed appropriate for annual data. The figures for world income were taken from the International Financial Statistics. Output gap, world income and call rate were the exogenous variables in the model.

The two components of expenditure, developmental and non-developmental, were used to evaluate the multiplier effect. The figures for tax revenues for the state and central government taken separately. To estimate the multiplier for combined developmental and non-developmental expenditure, the tax revenue figures for the central and state governments were added together. Both central and state receipts included revenue from direct and indirect taxes. Out of its total receipts, the central government transferred a certain portion to the state. In the analysis, the central tax revenue took account of the net transfers made to the state. Conversely, the state's total tax revenue included a share it received from the central government. The variables in the RBI handbook were at current prices, except for GDP. The wholesale price index was used to deflate the variables to obtain figures at constant 2004 prices. The annual growth rate of the variables was calculated so that when the variables were used in a regression, the coefficient would provide elasticity. The structure for estimating the SVAR was:

$$
\begin{bmatrix} e_t^{\text{govt exp}} \\ e_t^{\text{GDP}} \\ e_t^{\text{tax}} \end{bmatrix} = \begin{bmatrix} 1 & 0 & 0 \\ C_{21} & 1 & 0 \\ 0 & C_{32} & 1 \end{bmatrix} \begin{bmatrix} \in_t^{\text{govt exp}} \\ \in_t^{\text{GDP}} \\ \in_t^{\text{tax}} \end{bmatrix}
$$

where e_t refers to unobserved structural shocks and ε_t refers to observed structural shocks. The restrictions imply that the effect of GDP on expenditure is zero; however, expenditure does affect GDP. It was assumed that the expenditure would impact GDP in the short term but not vice-a-versa. The impulse response of GDP to expenditure gives the elasticity. Elasticity (α) is divided by the ratio of developmental (or non-developmental) expenditure to GDP to obtain the responsiveness of the GDP with respect to expenditure. This impulse response was the impact multiplier in this context. Mathematically, the multiplier could be written as:

$$\Delta \text{GDP} / \Delta \text{EXP} = \alpha / (\text{EXP/GDP}) \tag{3.1}$$

where EXP could be developmental (or non-developmental) expenditure of the state or central government or a combination of the two.

In recent years, the reliance on SVARs for measuring the size of fiscal multipliers has gained prominence. SVARs address the problem of simultaneity while imposing minimum restrictions, also called identification schemes. The problem of endogeneity arises because the decision to pursue a particular fiscal policy depends upon the phase through which the economy is passing and the level of output. Similarly, a fiscal shock can affect the level of output. There are four main identification schemes that can be used to estimate fiscal multipliers: (1) the recursive approach (Sims, 1980), (2) the traditional SVAR analysis (Blanchard and Perotti, 2002; Perotti, 2008), (3) the sign restriction approach (Uhlig, 2005) and (4) the narrative approach

(Ramey and Shapiro, 1998). Caldara and Kamps (2008, 2012) showed that all schemes had a favourable effect on output in the context of the US economy. This chapter has used the Blanchard and Perroti identification scheme which puts government expenditure before GDP and taxes (Blanchard and Perotti, 2002; Yadav et al., 2012). It implies that there will be a contemporaneous impact of developmental and non-developmental expenditure but it will only affect the level of taxes after passing through GDP. The level of expenditure will also not be affected by the prevailing economic conditions. Although the Blanchard-Perroti technique requires high-frequency (quarterly) data, there are many advantages associated with the use of annual data (Beetsma et al., 2008), such as less seasonal relevance, anticipation effects and the correspondence of data to actual shocks.

The VAR model of n variables can be written as:

$$A_o Y_{i,t} = \sum_{k=1}^{n} A_k Y_{i,t-k} + e_{i,t}$$
(3.2)

where $Y_{i,t}$ is a vector of exogenous and endogenous variables, $e_{i,t}$ is a vector of structural shocks and k is the lag length. The reduced form can be written as:

$$Y_{i,t} = \sum_{k=1}^{n} B_k Y_{i,t-k} + \in_{i,t}$$
(3.3)

where $B_k = A_o^{-1} A_k$ and $\in_{i,t} = A_o^{-1} e_{i,t}$

The above equation can be solved using the Blanchard–Perroti identification scheme, assuming that there is no automatic feedback of output on government spending (Yadav et al., 2012). Six variables were considered for the empirical exercise: developmental, non-developmental and combined government expenditure central, state and combined tax revenue. GDP was considered as an endogenous variable, while global GDP, call rate and output gap were the exogenous variables. Standard diagnostic tools were used, including the augmented Dicky–Fuller test to check for stationarity, the Granger causality test to check the long-run relationship between the variables, the stability of VAR and the Lagrange multiplier test to check the autocorrelation. The lag structure was selected using both Akaike's and Schwarz's Bayesian information criteria. All analyses were performed in Stata 13.0.

4 RESULTS

A summary of the statistics of the key variables is provided in Table 3.1. One key result which stands out is the high variability in the expenditure of the government (developmental as well as non-developmental). Table 3.2 shows

Table 3.1 Summary statistics of key variables, 1990–2013

Variable	N	Mean	SD	Min	Max
GDP growth rate	24	6.5	2.1	1.4	9.6
Central tax revenue growth rate	24	6.6	8.8	−8.7	21.9
State tax revenue growth rate	24	7.3	4.4	−0.3	17.6
Combined tax revenue growth rate	24	13.9	12.1	−4.6	36.1
Call money rate	24	8.7	4.1	3.2	19.6
Central developmental expenditure growth rate	24	22.8	54.2	−45.9	152.3
State developmental expenditure growth rate	24	23.6	53.3	−41.7	160.0
Combined developmental expenditure growth rate	24	23.3	52.7	−41.7	153.5
Central non-developmental expenditure growth rate	24	24.4	57.1	−41.0	169.1
State non-developmental expenditure growth rate	24	25.7	56.4	−40.8	170.3
Combined non-developmental expenditure growth rate	24	25.4	57.5	−39.9	170.2
World income growth rate	24	2.2	1.5	−2.9	3.9
Output gap	24	0.1	2.7	−4.6	7.6

Table 3.2 Average developmental and non-developmental expenditure (INR crore), 1990–2013

Period	Developmental expenditure (in INR crores)			Non-development expenditure (in INR crores)		
	Overall	Central	State	Overall	Central	State
1990–2000	25.5	23.7	27.0	30.7	29.7	32.0
	(61.5)	(63.9)	(62.6)	(66.1)	(65.6)	(63.3)
2001–13	21.5	21.9	20.8	20.8	19.9	20.4
	(46.5)	(47.1)	(46.4)	(51.6)	(51.1)	(51.8)
Overall (1990–2013)	23.3	22.8	23.6	25.3	24.4	25.7
	(52.7)	(54.2)	(53.3)	(57.5)	(57.1)	(56.4)

Note: Figures in parenthesis are standard errors.

the trend in the growth rate of developmental and non-developmental expenditure during 1990–2013. The average growth rate of state developmental (23.6%) and non-development (25.7%) expenditure was higher than the central developmental (22.8%) and non-developmental (24.4%) expenditure. The average growth rate of developmental and non-developmental expenditure during 2001–13 was 21.5% and 20.8%, respectively, which was lower than the average growth rate of developmental (25.5%) and non-developmental expenditure (30.7%) during 1990–2000. However, these figures mask the important variations that occurred on an annual basis. The overall expenditure and the expenditure on different components is usually very high during economic crises (1993–94, 2000–01 and 2008–09).

The Granger causality test results are reported in Table 3.3. The null hypothesis of the test procedure was that the lagged coefficients of each of the endogenous variables (i.e. growth rate in development expenditure, GDP and tax revenue) equalled zero. The lagged effect of all the endogenous variables (the last row of each panel in Table 3.3) was also zero. The results show

Table 3.3 Granger causality test for the growth rate of developmental expenditure, GDP and tax revenue, 1990–2013

Equation	Excluded	Chi-square value	df	P
Combined DE growth rate	GDP growth rate	5.8	3	0.120
Combined DE growth rate	Combined TR growth rate	1.2	3	0.747
Combined DE growth rate	All	21.3	6	0.002
GDP growth rate	Combined DE growth rate	19.5	3	0.000
GDP growth rate	Combined TR growth rate	13.3	3	0.004
GDP growth rate	All	22.1	6	0.001
Combined TR growth rate	Combined TR growth rate	30.8	3	0.000
Combined TR growth rate	GDP growth rate	7.2	3	0.066
Combined TR growth rate	All	43.2	6	0.000
Centre DE growth rate	GDP growth rate	11.7	3	0.009
Centre DE growth rate	Central TR growth rate	5.3	3	0.153
Centre DE growth rate	All	20.7	6	0.002
GDP growth rate	Central DE growth rate	23.3	3	0.000
GDP growth rate	Central TR growth rate	19.1	3	0.000
GDP growth rate	All	29.1	6	0.000
Centre TR growth rate	Central DE growth rate	26.7	3	0.000
Centre TR growth rate	GDP growth rate	5.0	3	0.168
Centre TR growth rate	All	32.2	6	0.000
State DE growth rate	GDP growth rate	3.8	3	0.290
State DE growth rate	State TR growth rate	14.3	3	0.003
State DE growth rate	All	52.4	6	0.000
GDP growth rate	State DE growth rate	10.0	3	0.018
GDP growth rate	State TR growth rate	6.3	3	0.099
GDP growth rate	All	14.6	6	0.024
State TR growth rate	State DE growth rate	5.0	3	0.174
State TR growth rate	GDP growth rate	9.3	3	0.025
State TR growth rate	All	24.1	6	0.000

DE, Developmental expenditure; TR, tax revenue.

that the null hypothesis of no Granger causality of combined development expenditure, GDP growth rate and combined tax revenue growth rate cannot be rejected, as most of the results are significant at the 1% level. Similar results were observed for the central- and state-level variables for both developmental and non-developmental expenditure (Table 3.4). The upshot is that fiscal shocks in the form of developmental and non-developmental expenditure affect GDP.

Table 3.5 presents the results from the SVAR model. Increases in both developmental and non-developmental expenditure can positively affect

Table 3.4 Granger causality test for the growth rate of non-developmental expenditure, GDP and tax revenue, 1990–2013

Equation	Excluded	Chi-square value	df	P
Combined NDE growth rate	GDP growth rate	9.4	3	0.025
Combined NDE growth rate	Combined TR growth rate	2.3	3	0.520
Combined NDE growth rate	All	31.9	6	0.000
GDP growth rate	Combined NDE growth rate	17.9	3	0.000
GDP growth rate	Combined TR growth rate	12.8	3	0.005
GDP growth rate	All	20.4	6	0.002
Combined TR growth rate	Combined NDE growth rate	30.0	3	0.000
Combined TR growth rate	GDP growth rate	6.9	3	0.076
Combined TR growth rate	All	42.3	6	0.000
Centre NDE growth rate	GDP growth rate	23.8	3	0.000
Centre NDE growth rate	Centre TR growth rate	6.4	3	0.094
Centre NDE growth rate	All	38.2	6	0.000
GDP growth rate	Central NDE growth rate	20.2	3	0.000
GDP growth rate	Central TR growth rate	17.8	3	0.000
GDP growth rate	All	25.6	6	0.000
Centre TR growth rate	Central NDE growth rate	29.2	3	0.000
Centre TR growth rate	GDP growth rate	6.2	3	0.105
Centre TR growth rate	All	35.0	6	0.000
State NDE growth rate	GDP growth rate	3.5	3	0.325
State NDE growth rate	State TR growth rate	24.7	3	0.000
State NDE growth rate	All	88.9	6	0.000
GDP growth rate	State NDE growth rate	11.0	3	0.012
GDP growth rate	State TR growth rate	9.8	3	0.021
GDP growth rate	All	15.6	6	0.016
State TR growth rate	State NDE growth rate	4.2	3	0.236
State TR growth rate	GDP growth rate	11.4	3	0.010
State TR growth rate	All	22.9	6	0.001

NDE, Non-developmental expenditure; TR, tax revenue

Table 3.5 Econometric estimates based on SVARs and impact multipliers, 1990–2013

Expenditure	Domain	Expenditure elasticity[a] 1	Mean GDP 2	Mean expenditure 3	Expenditure/GDP 4 = 3/2	Multiplier 5 = 1 × 4
Developmental expenditure	Combined	0.014	2,963,827	76,614	0.026	0.530
	Central	0.015	2,963,827	37,612	0.013	1.213
	State	0.030	2,963,827	47,951	0.016	1.843
Non-developmental expenditure	Combined	0.015	2,963,827	59,103	0.020	0.748
	Central	0.014	2,963,827	39,472	0.013	1.034
	State	0.012	2,963,827	24,631	0.008	1.420

[a] Obtained from the SVAR equation.

GDP. The elasticity of GDP with respect to state developmental expenditure (0.030) was higher than the central elasticity (0.015). Conversely, the elasticity of the central non-developmental expenditure was higher (0.014) than the state elasticity (0.012). The multiplier for developmental expenditure was comparatively higher than non-developmental expenditure, which is consistent with similar studies and as reported for other developing countries. The elasticity was notably sensitive to changes in the number of lags.

5 DISCUSSION AND CONCLUSIONS

Governments incur expenditure for different purposes, and given the welfare concerns and budget constraints, it is critical to decide upon the optimal allocation of resources. The Indian government has previously reported high fiscal deficits and a debt burden. Given that India is an emerging market and the distribution of income is highly skewed, it becomes the responsibility of the government to create opportunities by providing the basic infrastructure and facilities while achieving fiscal consolidation. However, the issue is how to incur the expenditures in a manner that maximizes the multiplier effect. This chapter used the SVAR estimation technique to measure the multiplier effect of developmental and non-developmental expenditure on output using annual data for India during 1990–2013. The results indicate that the size of the government's expenditure multiplier varied with the type of expenditures at different government levels; for example, the multiplier for developmental and non-developmental expenditure was higher for the state government than for the central government. However, the results should be interpreted with care. Variation in the results occurs depending upon the frequency of data and the choice of technique, which were discussed previously. The higher multiplier for states is also noteworthy. Jain and Kumar (2013) argued that the central government was responsible for a larger number of programmes and covered a larger area, therefore its multiplier effect was smaller. The crowding-out effect is also higher in the central government as the state governments have to maintain financial prudence to receive financial assistance. Certain studies (Auerbach and Gorodnichenko, 2011; Bose and Bhanumurthy, 2013; Ilzetzki et al., 2013) observed a negative multiplier or a very low multiplier. The negative multiplier depends on conditions such as a flexible exchange rate regime, a high debt-to-GDP ratio, high openness, a fragile financial sector, a high output gap and the quality of expenditure. Given the cap on fiscal deficit, the revenue expenditure for India could be negative in case it crowds out capital expenditure Bose and Bhanumurthy (2013).

A number of studies have tried to estimate the multiplier in India (Bahal, 2017; Bose and Bhanumurthy, 2013; Goyal and Sharma, 2015; Jain and Kumar, 2013; Yadav et al., 2012). The majority of these studies found that capital expenditure had a larger long-run positive impact on output compared to revenue expenditure. The expenditure incurred by the state government also had a higher impact when compared to the central government expenditure. Capital expenditure has the potential to reduce inflation volatility by reducing the structural bottlenecks (Goyal and Sharma, 2015). The results of this study also support this claim. However, the share of capital expenditure has decreased sharply, particularly over the boom period (2003–07) (Goyal and Sharma, 2015). At an institutional level, the composition of expenditure needs to change from being in favour of revenue expenditure to being in favour of capital expenditure. Building capacity can produce long-term externalities and push up future momentum by reducing supply bottlenecks. This, in turn, will have favourable effects on inflation and will create conditions for higher growth. Mundle et al. (2011) projected a growth rate of 8%, providing that the capital expenditure target of 6%, envisaged by the FRBM Act, is achieved alongside the zero-revenue deficit. Although the government has been promptly trying to eliminate the revenue deficit, the financial crisis of 2008 marred their efforts.

The majority of studies that have used SVAR have used quarterly data for estimation. The unavailability of reliable quarterly data for expenditure variables over a long period of time compelled us to use annual data, and the use of low-frequency data has been justified by Beetsma et al. (2008). Firstly, the concern of seasonality becomes less important when using annual data. Secondly, fiscal revisions are mostly performed on an annual basis, therefore it may be difficult to explain the association between fiscal shocks and quarterly data. Annual data may better reflect the effect of a fiscal shock. Thirdly, the anticipation effects become less significant when using annual data. However, annual data is not without its drawbacks. The use of annual data implies that fewer observations are available for the estimation of parameters; however, as long as the number of observations is greater than the number of parameters to be estimated, there is no issue. Another limitation is that the effect of output on public expenditure is not being identified within the same quarter; however, this is in favour of the identification scheme proposed in this study. Also, because the expenditure is budgeted on an annual basis, it makes sense to assume that government expenditure does not respond to output within a year. This study used the Blanchard–Perroti scheme that has been widely used in the Indian context; however, it will be useful to further verify the estimated multiplier using other alternative approaches.

The sensitivity of the multiplier with respect to the method of estimation and the prevailing conditions (i.e. trade openness, debt burden and capital mobility) has made this issue the holy grail of public expenditure effect. The results from this study are in line with the earlier studies on this subject. The multiplier effect of state developmental and non-developmental expenditure was higher than that of the central developmental and non-developmental expenditure. Given the fiscal scenario in the country, it is imperative to understand the effect of multipliers so that economic goals can be achieved without jeopardizing the fiscal space. In this regard, further research should be carried out to ascertain the effect of expenditure on economic and social services output, which are key items of the development expenditure. The multiplier effect of capital expenditure was higher than revenue expenditure, therefore it will be important to observe whether capital expenditure on these services is comparatively higher than revenue expenditure. Given the significant structural changes in the Indian economy, it will also be critical to comprehend the multipliers in both the pre- and post-liberalisation period to observe any differences due to fixed exchange rate regimes, capital immobility and trade restrictions.

The optimal allocation of resources poses a challenge to policymakers as India is grappling with both poverty and unemployment. The results from this study showed that the share of non-developmental expenditure has fallen during the last decade when compared to developmental expenditure. However, there is further scope to substitute non-developmental expenditure which could free up capital for investment in priority sectors such as health, education, agriculture and infrastructure. Investment of this nature could lead to an increase in labour productivity which could translate into higher savings. For example, saving rates were higher during the high growth phase of the last decade. Therefore investing in activities that can increase income as well as savings through the multiplier effect could be conducive to augmenting private investment and economic growth. This may also ensure that excessively stringent policy measures to curb fiscal deficits may not be necessary and can permit much needed fiscal space for social security and welfare.

APPENDIX: HODRICK–PRESCOTT FILTER

We have a time series for GDP, say yt, it could be written as sum of a growth component (g_t) and a cyclical component (c_t), such that

$$y_t = g_t + c_t$$

The cyclical component is the deviation from the growth component and its average is near zero. We can estimate a smoothed series by minimizing the following:

$$\sum_{t=1}^{T}(y_t - g_t)^2 + \lambda \sum_{t=2}^{T-1}[(g_{t+1} - g_t) - (g_t - g_{t-1})]^2$$

λ controls the smoothness of the series and penalizes the variability in the growth component, it is assumed 100 for annual series and 1600 for quarterly data.

REFERENCES

Alumnia, M., Benetrix, A., Eichengreen, B., O'Rourke, K., Rua, G., 2010. From Great Depression to Great Credit Crisis: Similarities, Differences and Lesson. Econ. Policy 25, 219–265.

Auerbach, A.J., Gorodnichenko, Y., 2011. Fiscal Multipliers in Recession and Expansion. NBER Working Papers 17447.

Bahal, G., 2017. Estimating Transfer Multiplier using spending on rural development programmes in India. Cambridge Working Papers in Economics.

Barro, R., 2009. Government spending is no free lunch. Wall St. J. A.17, (New York, N.Y.).

Barro, R.J., Redlick C.J., 2009. Macroeconomic Effects From Government Purchases and Taxes. NBER Working Paper No. 15369.

Bhattacharya, B.B., 1984. Public Expenditure, Inflation and Growth: A Macro-Econometric Analysis for India. Oxford University Press, Delhi.

Beetsma, R., Giuliodori, M., Klaasen, F., 2008. The effects of public spending shocks on trade balances in the European Union. J. Eur. Econ. Assoc. 6, 414–423.

Blanchard, O., Leigh, D., 2013. Growth forecast errors and fiscal multipliers. Am. Econ. Rev. 103, 117–120.

Blanchard, O., Perotti, R., 2002. An empirical characterisation of the dynamic effects of changes in government spending and taxes on output. Q. J. Econ. 117, 1329–1368.

Bose S., Bhanumurthy, N.R., 2013. Fiscal Multipliers for India. NIPFP Working Paper No. 125.

Caldara, D., Kamps, C., 2008. What are the Effects of Fiscal Shocks? A VAR-Based Comparative Analysis. European Central Bank Working Paper 877.

Caldara, D., Kamps, C., 2012. The Analytics of SVARs: A Unified Framework to Measure Fiscal Multipliers. Finance and Economics Discussion Series 2012–20.

Christiano, L., Eichenbaum, M., Rebelo, S., 2011. When is the government spending multiplier large? J. Polit. Econ. 119, 78–121.

Devarajan, S., Swaroop, V., Zou, H., 1996. The composition of public expenditure and economic growth. J. Monet. Econ. 37, 313–344.

Devereux, M.B., 2010. Fiscal Deficits, Debt, and Monetary Policy in a Liquidity Trap. Central Bank of Chile Working Paper No. 581.

Fatas, A., Mihov, I., 2001. The Effects of Fiscal Policy on Consumption and Employment: Theory and Evidence. CEPR Discussion Paper 2760.

Goyal, A., Sharma, B., 2015. Government Expenditure in India: Composition, Cyclicality and Multipliers. Indira Gandhi Institute of Development Research, Mumbai Working Papers.

Hicks, J.R., 1950. A Contribution to the Theory of the Trade Cycle. Clarendon Press, Oxford.

Ilzetzki, E., Mendoza, E., Végh, C., 2013. How big (small?) are fiscal multipliers? J. Monet. Econ. 60, 239–254.

Jain, R., Kumar, P., 2013. Size of Government Expenditure Multipliers in India: A Structural VAR Analysis. RBI Working Paper Series 7.

Kahn, R.F., 1931. The relation of home investment to unemployment. Econ. J. 41 (162), 173–198.

Keynes, J.M., 1936. The General Theory of Employment, Interest and Money, Book III, (Chapter 10). Macmillan & Co. Ltd., London.

Koh, W.C., 2017. Fiscal multipliers: new evidence from a large panel of countries. Oxf. Econ. Pap. 69 (3), 569–590.

Krishnamurty, K., 1985. Inflation and Growth: A model for India in Krishnamurty, K., and Pandit, V. Macroeconometric Modelling of the Indian Economy: Studies on Inflation and Growth. Hindustan Publishing House, Delhi.

Landau, D.L., 1986. Government and economic growth in the less developed countries: an empirical study for 1960–88. Econ. Dev. Cult. Change 35, 35–75.

Miller, S.M., Russek, F.S., 1997. Fiscal structures and economic growth. Econ. Inq. 35, 603–613.

Mundle, S., Bhanumurthy, N.R., Das, S., 2011. Fiscal consolidation with high growth: a policy simulation model for India. Econ. Model. 28, 2657–2668.

Perotti, R., 1999. Fiscal policy in good times and bad. Q. J. Econ. 114, 1399–1436.

Perotti, R., 2005. Estimating the Effects of Fiscal Policy in OECD Countries. CEPR Discussion Papers, No. 4842. Centre for Economic Policy Research, London.

Perotti, R., 2008. In search of the transmission mechanism of fiscal policy. NBER Mcroeconomics Annual 2007. 22, MIT, Cambridge, Mass, pp. 169–226, Daron Acemaglou, Kenneth Rogoff and Michael Woodford.

Ram, R., 1986. Government size and economic growth: a new framework and some evidence from cross-section and time series data. Am. Econ. Rev. 76, 191–203.

Ramey, V.A., Shapiro, M.D., 1998. Costly Capital Reallocation and the Effects of Government Spending. Carnegie-Rochester Conference Series on Public Policy 48. , (June): 145194.

Romer, P., 1989. What Determines the Rate of Growth and Technological Change. World Bank Working Papers.

Romer, P.M., 1990a. Human capital and growth: theory and evidence. Carnegie–Rochester Conference Series on Public Policy 40, 47–57.

Romer, P.M., 1990b. Capital, Labour and Productivity. Brookings Papers on Economic Activity, Special Issue, 337-420.

Sims, C.A., 1980. Macroeconomics and reality. Econometrica 48 (1), 148.

Snowdown, B., Vane, H.R., 2005. Modern Macroeconomics: Its Origins, Development and Current State. E. Elgar, Cheltenham.

State Finances, 2009-10. A Study of Budgets of 2009–10. Annual Publication, Reserve Bank of India.

Tobin, J., 1987. Policies for Prosperity: Essays in a Keynesian Mode. Jackson, P.M. (ed.), Brighton: Wheatsheaf.

Tobin, J., An overview of the General Theory. Cowles Foundation Paper No. 947.

Uhlig, H., 2005. What are the effects of monetary policy on output? Results from an agnostic identification procedure. J. Monet. Econ. 52 (2), 381–419.

Woodford, M., 2011. Simple analytics of the government expenditure multiplier. Am. Econ. J. Macroecon. 3, 1–35.

Yadav, S., Upadhyay, V., Sharma, S., 2012. Impact of fiscal policy shocks on the Indian economy. Margin J. Appl. Econ. Res. 6 (4), 415–444.

FURTHER READING

Hodrick, R.J., Edward, C.P., 1997. Postwar U.S. business cycles: an empirical investigation. J. Money Credit Bank. 29 (1), 1–16.

IMF, 2012. World Economic Outlook: Coping with High Debt and Sluggish Growth.

Miguel, A., Benetrix, A., Eichengreen, B., Rourke, K., Rua, G., 2010. From great depression to great credit crisis: similarities, differences and lessons. Econ. Policy 25.

Perotti, R., 2007. In Search of the Transmission Mechanism of Fiscal Policy. NBER Working Paper 131–143.

Reserve Bank of India, 2016. Handbook of Statistics on the Indian Economy, 2016–17.

CHAPTER 4

Failing to Learn: India's Schools and Teachers

Bibhas Saha*, Shreyosi Saha**
*Durham University Business School, Durham, United Kingdom
**University of Cambridge, Cambridge, United Kingdom

1 INTRODUCTION

Since the turn of the new millennium, India has made substantial progress in universalising primary education. They enacted the Right to Education Act and committed substantial resources to building more schools, hiring new teachers and providing school meals under the Education for All (*Sarva Shiksha Abhiyan*) campaign. Most villages now have a school within a 1 km radius. The gross enrolment rate at primary school level is now 100% for both boys and girls. Even for minorities and disadvantaged communities, such as scheduled castes (SC) and scheduled tribes (ST), the enrolment rate is rapidly improving.

While this is a great achievement, it has also brought about new questions; for example, are the children learning what they are supposed to learn? Are they going to stay in education until the end of high school or are they going to drop out before that? These questions are very important for several reasons: Firstly, these children account for roughly one-seventh of India's population and they are going to enter the labour force in 10–12 years from now. They are likely to face global competition, particularly from East Asian children, whose learning level is much higher. Secondly, a less cheerful picture emerges when scrutinising secondary education, as the government initiatives in the new millennium could not prevent the high drop-out rate (more so for girls than boys) that has remained a constant feature over the last few decades. Thirdly, income inequality is rising in India, much of it along the axis of skills and education. This skills gap must not be allowed to widen further if inequality is to be contained.

This chapter focussed on several issues, including whether private schools educate children to a higher level than public schools. How teachers can be incentivised to perform more efficiently to produce enhanced learning environments? How early schooling (preschool) can boost student

Changing the Indian Economy
http://dx.doi.org/10.1016/B978-0-08-102005-0.00004-6

learning in later years, and why high drop-out rates are observed amongst older children, particularly near the end of the secondary schooling? And how this problem can be addressed to universalise secondary schooling?

Section 2 will provide some facts and figures on the state of learning at primary level and the drop-out rate statistics. Section 3 will discuss some of the findings from the literature regarding the efficiency of private schools and the effects of incentivising teachers. Section 4 will address relatively old literature on returns to education, where insight will be gained into the substitutability between early work and finishing school. Some recent studies will also be discussed here. Finally, the scope of the New Education Policy will be highlighted in the concluding remarks.

2 INDIA'S LEARNING OUTCOMES

The learning outcome of a nation must be reflected by the literacy levels, and over time in adult literacy. Of course, literacy is not enough in modern times, and a primary school child must now have a basic skill set in both numeracy and literacy, which should include some elementary knowledge of English. Subsequent skills are expected to be built in secondary schools. However, as high levels of poverty persisted in India until the 1980s, early efforts to push primary education did not achieve much success. It was only after poverty levels began to fall in the 1990s that educational progress began to accelerate; however, the overall picture since independence is a series of missed opportunities.

2.1 Literacy, Drop-Out Rates and Not-in-School Children

Literacy is one low-hanging fruit that should not have been missed. The literacy rate in 1951 was a mere 18.3%; however, this had risen to 73% in 2011, roughly rising by <1% per year. This increase was slow compared to countries such as China, Malaysia, Vietnam and Sri Lanka, all of which have raised their literacy rates close to 100%, although their literacy rates were comparable to or even lower than India's for a few decades. The current progress rate suggests that it is likely to take another 30 years to achieve universal literacy.

However, even the 73% literacy rate hides some ugly facts, such as the enormous gender disparity in literacy. In the 2011 census, the literacy rate was 80.9% for males and 64.6% for females. Since 1951, the literacy rates for males and females have risen by 53.7% and 55.7%, respectively. Another important point is that 3%–4% of the gain in literacy comes from the 7–15 age group, who are yet to enter the labour force. The adult (>15 years) literacy rate in India is 69.3%; however, among the STs, the adult literacy rate is substantially behind other population groups at just 51.9%.[a]

A clear reason for slow progress in literacy rates is that many children are not engaged at school. Although almost all are enrolled, many drop out early and lose their literacy skills thereafter. It is important to distinguish between 'dropouts' and 'not-in-school' children. The official drop-out data are annual figures that cover only those who do not complete their respective level of education out of the in-school cohort. Children that dropped out earlier or who never attended school need to be counted separately by looking at the gross enrolment ratio, which compares the enrolment figures with the population figure for that age group. As per the 2013–14 data on dropouts, roughly 4%–5% of children dropped out at the primary stage, and nearly 18% dropped out at the secondary stage. Therefore if 100 students started out at grade 1, 75.57 students would be estimated to complete their secondary education, while the remaining 24.43 children would drop out at various stages, mostly around grade 9.[b]

Dropout data were not collected systematically in the past, therefore it is not possible to establish whether there has been a marked decline in the drop-out rate compared to a decade ago; however, time series data on gross enrolment are available, which may be used to provide a picture of not-in-school children. These data show that all primary school age (6–10 years) children have been enrolled in schools since 2005–06; however, for the upper primary group (10–13 years), 91.2% children were in school in 2014–15 compared to only 71% in 2005–06. Therefore there was a marked 20.2% improvement over a 9-year period, and the bulk of this gain was for girls (almost 30%). At the secondary level (14–15 years), the enrolment rate improved from 52.2% in 2005–06 to 78.5% in 2014–15. Girls also registered greater gains in this category, increasing from 46.2% to 78.9%. Although this represents a remarkable improvement, 21.5% of children aged 13 and 14 are still not in school.

While the gross enrolment data and dropout data are not directly comparable, they seem to be consistent. ASER (2016) (p. 51) estimated that 15.3% of rural children aged 15–16 and 4.6% aged 11–14 were not in school. Therefore it is not unreasonable to suggest that at least 20%–25% of

[a] Education statistics at a glance (Government of India, 2016a).
[b] This is estimated by the authors based on Table 10 (p. 8) and Table 25 (p. 36) of Education Statistics at a Glance 2016 (Government of India, 2016a).

children would have <10 years of education. This is despite government's initiative to retain students in school and make education accessible to all children up to the age of 15.

It is noteworthy that the enrolment data for girls is higher than for boys at both upper primary and secondary stages. This overtaking by the girls has occurred over the last 5 years and is also supported by the drop out data. Therefore one intriguing question is why girls are staying in school longer than boys, and this will be addressed later in the chapter.

In summary, India has made steady but slow progress with regards to literacy and has committed great resources to expanding education facilities to wider populations. However, challenges remain in retaining children at school and inspiring them to continue to the secondary level. The enrolment of girls in school and their continuation in school has improved to a greater extent than boys; however, questions still remain such as what is learnt at school? This will be the focus of the following section.

2.2 Learning

Historically, there were no systematic surveys for assessing student learning, and nothing could be ascertained about the level of learning until the secondary school competition exam, which was too late. There are now two available surveys that are conducted on a regular basis. The first survey is organised by the government-run National Council of Education Research and Training (NCERT) and is called National Achievement Survey (NAS). It involves testing grade V students on their language, maths and environmental knowledge using a pen and paper in a school setting. Four cycles of the NAS have been completed since 2001, and the latest survey conducted in 2014 covering 150,101 students in 8266 schools across 34 states and union territories.

The other survey is called the Annual Status of Education Report (ASER) and is conducted by the education non-governmental organisation (NGO) Pratham. The main aim of ASER is to generate estimates of the basic reading and arithmetic abilities of children aged 5–16. It also assesses the schooling status of children aged 3–16. The test is conducted at the household level as part of its annual education survey. The coverage of ASER has been steadily growing; in 2016 the survey was carried out in 17,473 villages in 589 districts, covering 350,232 households and 562,305 children aged 3–16.[c]

---

[c] The coverage of ASER has been steadily growing. In 2012 it reached 331,490 households in 568 districts, surveyed 595,139 children aged 3–16 and assessed 448,467 children aged 5–16.

The NAS test and the ASER test are very different in terms of their design, purpose and scope. The NAS is elaborately designed to map students' achievement onto a common national scale. It is good at creating a distribution of scores for every state surveyed, and thus it describes a state's relative position in terms of the overall average and each percentile point of the score distribution. In contrast, the ASER design is simple and its results are easy to interpret. The most important aspect of the ASER test is that it describes whether the student can demonstrate knowledge of basic principles that every primary school child should learn. The focus of ASER is to reveal the learning deficit in underperforming students.

Some interesting facts emerged from the latest NAS (2015) report. For example, girls performed better than boys. There was no significant disparity between rural and urban India with respect to performance. SC and ST children continued to perform below other children. However, more worryingly, the average performance recorded in 2014 (cycle 4) was lower than that recorded in 2010 (cycle 3).

ASER (2016) presents a different aspect of the learning deficiency. Their tests generally ask students to perform certain literacy and numeracy tasks that they should have learnt several years earlier. Failing to perform these tasks reveals how deficient they are relative to a minimum standard expected in their age groups. General findings from ASER (2016) show that there were some improvements in the reading ability of primary school level children between 2014 and 2016; however, at higher levels of schooling there was no improvement in either literacy or numeracy, and, if anything, the situation had worsened in the 13–14 age group.

Table 4.1, which was taken from ASER (2016) (p. 52), illustrates the poor state of learning in rural India. For example, only 9.8% of students in grade I met or exceeded the expectation of being able to read grade I text or grade II text.[d] The remaining 90.2% of grade I students failed the reading test, and 46.1% of these could not identify letters or the alphabet. The picture was not any better for older children either. Only 13.4% of grade II students could read grade II texts. The percentage of children not able to read beyond grade I text ranged from 17.3% to 19.2% amongst students in grades III to IV. Even amongst eighth graders, 13.0% of students were unable to read grade I text. However, as Table 4.2 shows, this picture is improving over time in both public and private schools.

---

[d] The highest level of text students were given was grade II.

Table 4.1 Percentage distribution of learning deficient children in rural India

Currently studying in grade	Could not identify letters	At most identified letters	At most read words	At most read Grade I text	Could read Grade II text	Total
I	46.1	31.7	12.4	5.0	4.8	100
II	23.5	31.5	19.8	11.8	13.4	100
III	13.6	24.1	19.9	17.3	25.1	100
IV	8.5	17.2	17.7	19.2	37.4	100
V	6.0	13.3	14.2	18.6	47.8	100
VI	4.0	9.6	11.6	18.0	56.9	100
VII	2.8	7.2	8.9	15.1	66.1	100
VIII	2.0	5.4	6.5	13.0	73.0	100

Source: ASER, 2016. Annual Status of Education Report (Rural) 2016. Available from: www.asercentre.org., p. 52.

Table 4.2 Trends in reading ability

	Grade III children who could read grade II text		
Year	Government school (%)	Private school (%)	Weighted average (%)
2010	16.8	29.7	19.6
2012	16.7	33.8	21.5
2014	17.2	37.8	23.6
2016	19.3	38.0	25.2

Source: ASER, 2016. Annual Status of Education Report (Rural) 2016. Available from: www.asercentre.org., p. 52.

A more detailed picture on numeracy and the state-wise breakdown can be found in ASER reports. However, the general picture is that student achievements fell short of the curriculum expectation by a large margin. Therefore it is not unfair to say that Indian children are 2–3 years behind their peers in developed countries and East Asian economies.

3 HOW TO IMPROVE LEARNING?

One obvious question is why do children fail to learn? Is it because our public schools are simply not doing their job? At first glance, learning deficiencies appear to be far less common amongst students attending private schools (Table 4.2), although both schools do share this issue. If private schools are better, then should the government encourage more private schools?

It could be argued that some of the key efficiency features in private schools could be replicated in public schools by altering the learning and teaching methods and by incentivising the teachers; however, to what extent can public schools be reformed? Another issue is when to start schooling. Are children starting too late in their schooling? Evidence suggests that an early education does matters; however, government schools do not currently have kindergarten sections. Therefore should the government change its policy? The following section discusses some of these issues in more depth.

3.1 Private Versus Public Schools

The last few decades have witnessed a significant expansion of the global private education sector due to the realisation that the private sector can be an effective provider of public goods. Private schools are no longer seen as elite institutions patronised only by the rich. In a global report, EdInvest (2000) (pp. 5–7) identified six types of private schools in developing countries that ranged from very inexpensive schools run primarily for poor children by charitable organizations and NGOs to highly expensive international boarding schools catering to the rich. Tooley and Dixon (2003) provided an early account of private schools in India that catered to the poor and to those that could not be accommodated in government schools due to strict regulations. ASER (2016) reported that approximately 30% of children go to private schools in rural India and in urban India, this figure increases to 50%–65%.

Ignoring the diversity in the private education sector that is typical in developing countries, one question that may be asked is: are private schools better than public schools? This question goes to the heart of another debate over whether private schools are truly better schools, or whether they look better because they attract better students. The answer to the question rests on whether the school's contribution to the student's performance can be sufficiently separated from the student's own contribution (i.e. due to their higher ability). The best way to avoid the school selection bias, which is caused by the student's ability or their desire to enjoy a better peer effect and to associate with children from similar socioeconomic groups, is to randomise the student admission process; however, admission is rarely decided through randomisation. The literature on school efficiencies has dealt with the selection issue in a number of ways, and recent work has been shown to be much more reliable at providing a better treatment of the school selection bias.

Despite their differences in the treatment of the selection bias, most studies tended to agree that private schools were more efficient than public schools; this evidence seems to be robust for developed countries but less so for developing countries. The superiority of the private schools also seems to vary depending on the student achievement measure and the level of education (primary or secondary). For early literature see Jimenez and Lockheed (1991) and Kingdon (1996), and for more recent work see Desai et al. (2008), Pal (2010) and Muralidharan and Sundraraman, (2015).

However, there are some prominent exceptions that dispute the superiority of private schools. For example, Newhouse and Beegle (2006) studied the performance of Indonesian school children in grades 7–9 and found that public schools were more efficient than private schools. The authors attributed the public-school success to the unobserved higher quality inputs used. Using surveys across 10 Latin American countries, Somers et al. (2004) also found no significant private-school effect on a child's performance once the household, student and peer-group characteristics were accounted for. This was consistent with the findings of another Latin American study in which McEwan and Carnoy (2000) examined a 1980 voucher programme in Chile to determine its effects on the growth of for-profit private schools, church schools and public schools. After controlling for various factors, the study found that public schools were relatively more efficient than for-profit private schools.

In India, several studies have recently attempted to identify the private school effects. Chudgar and Quin (2012) analysed the India Human Development Survey (IHDS) 2005 data for a sample of 7000 rural children and 3000 urban children. The survey contained detailed information on individual and household characteristics alongside scores in maths, reading and writing. The authors applied the propensity score matching technique to correct for the school selection bias. Once the selection bias was corrected (by this method) and all other observable characteristics were controlled for, there was no longer any private school effect and the children performed identically regardless of whether they attended a private school or a public school or whether they lived in a village or town. The authors also highlighted that low-fee private schools that lure low-income families away from public schools do not provide better education, contrary to the popular perception.

Two recent studies from Andhra Pradesh have addressed the school selection bias in the best possible way and hence their estimates are the most reliable (Muralidharan and Sundraraman, 2015; Singh, 2015).

In 2008, Muralidharan and Sundraraman (2015) conducted a two-tier experiment regarding school admission in 180 villages in Andhra Pradesh involving over 10,000 households. Each village was carefully chosen to ensure that there was at least one public school and one private school in the village. Parents of public-school children were invited to apply for a voucher that would enable their children to switch to a private school, and the cost of doing so would also be covered by the voucher.[e] After receiving the applications for vouchers, the authors ran two lotteries. The first lottery determined which villages would act as the control villages ($n = 90$) and which villages would act as the treatment villages ($n = 90$). Treatment meant that the voucher programme would be offered, and control meant that the voucher would not be offered. A second lottery was then conducted in the treatment villages to determine which applicants would get the voucher. Voucher winners then exercised their choice to move to a private school (within a treatment village). The experimental design mimicked a programme of random assignment in school admissions that would avoid school selection bias. In addition, the careful creation of a control group, where some people wanted to receive the voucher but could not have it because the treatment did not take place, allowed for comparisons to be drawn with the treatment group so that any peer effect of the voucher programme could be detected.[f] The academic performance of the students was tracked for 4 years to generate a panel dataset. This is probably the cleanest dataset one could attain from the field.

The authors found that there was no private school effect in most subjects (i.e. Telegu, maths, English, science and social studies). The only effect was observed for Hindi, which is generally not taught in public schools in Andhra Pradesh. However, the private schools were less costly due to the lower salaries of the teachers, therefore private schools could be regarded as better as they produced the same outcome at a lower cost. The findings from this carefully controlled study in Andhra Pradesh in 2008 were not dissimilar to those reported by Chudgar and Quin (2012) from a 2005 national database (for a very different type of test scores).

Singh (2015) used a different dataset in the same state that was collected under the Young Lives project between 2002 and 2011. Young Lives

---

[e] Participating private schools did not have any discretion to deny admission to voucher recipients if places were available.

[f] The peer effect can change due to the entry of new students or the exit of old students that was induced by the vouchers.

was a longitudinal study of child poverty in Ethiopia, India (only Andhra Pradesh), Peru and Vietnam. The survey tracked two cohorts of children: the first consisted of 1008 children born between January 1994 and June 1995 and the second consisted of 2011 children born between January 2001 and June 2002. The educational data and test performances of the children were analysed to estimate the private-school effect after controlling for the time-varying and time-invariant effects. The author used the value-added model to refine the private-school effects by netting out persistence or the decay of learning. The authors observed that there were a strong private-school effect for English, a mixed effect for Telegu and no effect for maths; English medium private schools performed worse than public schools for Telegu.

There are a great variety of private schools in India, and the low-fee private schools offer serious competition to underperforming public schools. Some private schools are organised by philanthropists and charities, while others could be profit-motivated (although all are typically registered as non-profit organisations, as Indian law states that all schools must be non-profit). Therefore it would be worthwhile to assess if the two types of private schools could be distinguished and if they differ in efficiency. If socially-motivated schools perform better, there is a strong case for nurturing this segment of the private sector.

Pal and Saha (2017b) attempted this comparison in Nepal using two national surveys on school leaving certificate (SLC) exam data from 2002 to 2004. Nepal passed a unique amendment to its Nepal Education Act 2028 in 1992, which gave scope for private investment in education. The Act allowed a private school to be registered as a non-profit trust or a profit-making company. A registered company was given a free hand in setting the school fees but was liable for taxation on any profit and it was not allowed to receive any public subsidy at any stage. Conversely, a trust was subjected to multiple regulations. Furthermore, any private school that had received any private donations or public subsidies in the past was required to be registered as a trust. This regulatory intervention made it difficult for private schools to use the trust tag as a disguise to make a profit. Therefore their separation in terms of their registered status corresponds fairly to their true behaviour.

Pal and Saha (2017b) observed that the trust schools were a small minority that were often set up and run by philanthropists, educationists and NGOs. They were generally English medium and on average more expensive than public schools; however, they were not as expensive as the company schools. The authors used the instrumental variable approach to correct for school selection bias and found that, in terms of the students'

SLC marks, the trust schools were the best schools in Nepal. This was followed by the profit-seeking company schools and finally the public schools. Students from trust schools outperformed all other students. The authors concluded that the private provision of education should be guided by social motivation rather than profits.

3.2 Teacher Incentives and Student Performance

The role of the teacher in public schools often receives global public attention for both the right and wrong reasons. Education forms a big part of election campaigns in Western countries; for example, former US president George W. Bush launched the 'No Child Left Behind' campaign, pledging to drastically overhaul the public education programme. At a similar time, the UK Government ran its 'Every Child Matters' campaign. In India, politicians and parents often take matters regarding disciplining 'erring' teachers into their own hands. One of the widely-observed problems in the developing world is teacher absenteeism (Chaudhury et al., 2006). The absenteeism can take the form of unreported absences, unofficially working for fewer hours or simply not performing the work sincerely despite being present in class.

A natural way to address teacher absenteeism is to alter the incentives for teachers. Teachers are generally paid either a fixed salary or a salary linked to their hours of work. They are supposed to be supervised by the school's headteacher and inspected randomly by an external agency. Therefore incentives typically take the form of a negative reward, (i.e. non-compliance leading to some sort of punishment). The incentive literature suggests that a fixed salary and job security are both vulnerable to a teacher's moral hazard. Although negative incentives can be effective, they usually do not ensure the quality aspect of work. Positive rewards (i.e. a bonus) are more effective in this regard.

The use of a fixed-salary scheme combined with a punishment scheme that is not efficiently pursued should be reviewed. Two methods of altering the incentives are to change the job tenures or to give a positive 'reward' for better test results. Similar experiments have been tried in many countries, notably in the United States; however, the results were mixed and included the possibility of teacher's cheating (Levitt and Dubner, 2005, pp. 19–54).

A number of Indian studies have explored this question in detail using the randomized control trial (RCT) method. These experiments are naturally small scale and therefore it is not easy to generalise their findings to the whole country; however, insights gained from these experiments are important building blocks for state-level and national policies. The following section discusses three such experiments.

The first study was performed by Muralidharan and Sundararaman (2011). The authors conducted a large-scale randomized experiment in Andhra Pradesh using a sample of 500 public schools, of which 100 constituted the control group. The remaining 400 schools were split between four different treatment groups (i.e. four different types of incentive reform), which were:

1. The schools were given bonuses based on the average maths and Telegu test scores
2. Individual teachers were given bonuses based on the average maths and Telegu test scores of their students.
3. Schools were given an extra contract teacher
4. Schools were given a cash grant for school materials

Treatments (1) and (2) were designed to address the incentive question and compare the outcomes of incentives given at a group level with those given at an individual level. Treatments (3) and (4) were intended to address if additional teaching resources or money, both of which are often cited as major problems, would affect the outcome. The experiment ran for 2 years, and student performance data were collected before and after the experiments as well as periodically during the experiment. Information on a host of other variables was also collected.

The main findings of this paper were very interesting. Firstly, the treatment schools performed better than the control schools in both maths and Telegu, with maths producing a quantitatively stronger effect. Secondly, in treatment schools, the post-treatment scores were higher than the pretreatment scores at every point on the score distribution. Thirdly, there were spillover effects to other subjects; for example, science and social studies were not subjected to treatment but registered improved student scores in the treatment schools. Fourthly, individual incentive schools (treatment 2) outperformed the group incentive schools (treatment 1) after 2 years of the programme, thus suggesting that individual incentives are more efficient than group incentives. Fifthly, the treatments did not influence teacher attendance but induced greater and more effective teaching efforts. As expected, incentives worked on both the quality and quantity dimensions of work, but absenteeism is likely to require a different solution. Finally, extra contract teachers and cash grants were not as effective and were more expensive programmes than the incentive schemes.

The second study was performed by Duflo et al. (2012). The authors used a RCT and monitoring method to investigate how absenteeism and learning outcomes were improved by financial incentives. The experiment was conducted over a period of 4 years (starting from September 2003) in a network of non-formal schools in Western India run by the NGO, Seva Mandir. The treatment and control groups each contained 57 schools. The baseline teacher attendance data were collected in August 2003, and this was then compared with the data collected during the treatment period. The treatment schools received the following incentives:

- Each school was provided with a camera and students were instructed to take pictures of the teacher and other students at the start and end of the school day.
- The cameras noted the date and time and were tamperproof; a valid day was classed as 5 hours between the 'start' and 'end' photo.
- There was a non-linear payment structure where teachers received a INR 500 fine if they attended fewer than 10 days in each month. They also received INR 50 for any additional day attended that month (from the 10th day onwards).
- Another way to view the payment structure is as a base salary of INR 1000 for at least 20 days work/month, a bonus of INR 50 for each extra day after the 20th day and a INR 50 fine for each skipped day in the first 20 days (capped at INR 500).

In contrast, the teachers at control schools received a fixed salary of INR 1000/month without any monitoring, but they were reminded that regular presence was a requirement of their job.

The results of this experiment were very encouraging. Firstly, the programme systematically improved attendance. After 30 months, the absence rates of teachers in the treatment schools had dropped from 44% to 21%; the absence rate in the control schools was 42%. Secondly, teacher absence in the treatment schools fell across the whole distribution. Thirdly, the attendance improvement got stronger over time. After 4 years the teacher attendance was 72% in the treatment schools compared to 61% in the control schools. Fourthly, using a separate and structural model, the authors also estimated the elasticity of the labour supply with respect to the level of the financial bonus and found this estimate to be between 0.2 and 0.3. Finally, the students in the treatment school also benefitted from the programme. After 1 year, their test scores were significantly higher than their counterparts in the control schools. After 2.5 years, students in the treatment schools were 10% more likely to transfer to a formal primary school than their peers in the control schools.

The two studies discussed above focussed on teacher incentives and teacher absenteeism. However, there is also an issue of providing special attention to weaker students that cannot be addressed by incentivising the teachers to work more for the whole class. A specific intervention must be designed that is aimed at weaker students, and Banerjee et al. (2007) conducted one such RCT in Mumbai. The study also reported another RCT in Vadodara which looked at the role of computers as learning aids. Both experiments were run with the help of *Pratham*.

The Mumbai experiment (initiated in 1998) was a remedial education program for the weakest students in grades 3 or 4. Selected students were taken out of normal classrooms for 2 hours (out of a total class time of 4 hours) to work with a new supplementary teacher (a young woman called *Balsakhi*[g]) to learn basic skills.

The experiment produced some interesting results. Firstly, the remedial education program increased the average test scores in the treatment schools, and the impact was stronger in the second year of the treatment. The weakest students gained the most; however, the gains faded after the programme was discontinued. At 1 year after the programme finished, the gain in the scores of the low-scoring students fell quite a bit. Secondly, taking the weaker students out of the classroom for remedial teaching did not affect the performance of the remaining students.

The Vadodara experiment (initiated in 1999) offered children in grade 4 two hours of shared computer time per week, during which they were able to play computer games involving maths problems. The difficulty of the maths problems corresponded to their ability to solve them, and the programme was targeted at all students in the treatment schools.

As in the Mumbai experiment, students experienced a significant gain in the first year, which corresponded to an increase in their maths scores. There was also a further increase in the second year of the experiment; however, 1 year after the programme stopped, some of these reported gains began to fade. These results suggest that weaker students need to be given special assistance and that this assistance should be sustained over time.

3.3 Early Learning (Head Start)

Desai and Vanneman (2015) argued that children learn at different paces 'some are early achievers and others bloom late'. When analysing IHDS data they showed that only 10% of children who had severe learning deficiency early on in life (i.e. those who could not read simple words at age 8–11) could complete grade 9, compared to approximately 60% of children

---

[g] Balsakhi is also a remedial education programme run by the NGO Pratham.

who were not deficient in learning at the same age. Chaudhary and Kaul (2015) also raised some thought-provoking issues and evidence on school readiness in Indian children. The authors analysed longitudinal data on 2500 6-year-old children from Assam, Telangana and Rajasthan that had been collected by the Centre of Early Childhood Education and Development at Ambedkar University. They argued even 1 year of good-quality preschool education for disadvantaged children at age 4 or 5 could make a big difference to their learning at grade 1 and help their learning at age 7 and 8. They estimated that children gained an average of a third of a year of additional learning across language, reading and maths through good-quality preschool education. This finding is particularly important in view of the dire learning situation recorded by the ASER and NCERT surveys. The integration of 1–2 years of preschool education with primary education could drastically change the learning outcomes of primary education, toward which the government has made great efforts in the last two decades.

Access to adequate resources is an issue; however, cheaper alternatives may be available. Experts have suggested that the current system of Anganwadi, which monitors basic health care in rural children, could be expanded to include preschool education. There are also suggestions for using private preschool facilities (i.e. playschools and KG schools) and making them accessible to low-income families through subsidies. It is hoped that the New Education Policy will explore such options.

The benefits of early childhood schooling or a head start are felt not only in terms of the short-term gains (i.e. school readiness and test scores) but also in terms of long-term sociopsychological development. Numerous studies from the United States, including the High/Scope Perry Preschool Study (1962–65) in Ypsilanti, Michigan; The Abecedarian Project (1972–77) in Chapel Hill, North Carolina, and The Chicago Parent Center (analysis from 1983–85 cohort), in Chicago, all confirmed head start effects such as an IQ advantage and a higher academic performance at primary and early high school stages. Early childhood investment has an impact on cognitive ability immediately after the treatment but fades without further investment. However, the impacts of non-cognitive skills are sustained into later life, and early childhood investments result in a better adult life. Those children with a head start are more likely to complete school, commit less crime, not smoke and earn more money. For more information on the long-term impacts of early schooling see Carneiro and Ginja (2014), Currie and Thomas (1995, 2000) and Currie et al. (2002).

4 DEMAND-SIDE ISSUES

This chapter has so far addressed the supply-side issues (i.e. the right type of school, better teaching and the right age of education); however, the demand-side issues should not be overlooked. For example, what if the child (or their parents) do not see the value in education because there are high opportunity costs now and because the future returns to education are at best uncertain. This problem seems to be relevant to the 14–16 age group where the drop-out rate is particularly high (15%–20%).

It could be argued that better learning today will improve the labour productivity in adult life, which will, in turn, improve the job prospects and earning potential. This argument relies on the assumption of a positive slope of the earnings function, which seems to be empirically validated by hundreds of earnings studies conducted all over the world. Banerjee and Duflo (2011) (pp. 86–89) also argued that there cannot be an education trap nestled in a low education–low income loop alongside a high education–high income loop in a multiple equilibrium environment. However, poor people behave as if they are confronting a trap, as they not only terminate schooling prematurely, even when there are no direct costs, but they also take extreme risks by educating one child (usually a boy) at the expense of denying education to his siblings. Banerjee and Duflo (2011) speculate that this could be due to a behavioural disconnect between evidence and perception.

This section discusses the literature regarding the earnings function and some papers that have directly examined the school drop-out problem. Early earnings studies in India were severely constrained by the lack of disaggregate or household data. These studies utilised aggregates (district or village level) of earnings and education and found a declining rate of return profiles, thus indicating that primary education yields the highest rate of return to education. This was consistent with earning studies from other countries. Earning studies in the 1990s began to use more disaggregate data, and although they varied in terms of their area of coverage, most reported a substantially higher rate of return to college education than school education. For example, Saha and Sarkar (1999) utilised an industry level dataset on private sector workers and employees earning above a certain threshold. Interestingly, despite crossing a threshold income level, not all workers and employees were high school graduates. In fact, the education level varied from primary to university level, as did their work experience; however, there was often a significant gap in their recorded work experience, especially in those with a poor education. Careful examination of the data suggested that this gap was informal sector work experience that enabled poorly-educated individuals to gain entry to the formal sector and eventually earn a decent salary, albeit at a much higher age than those who had a higher education.

In their earnings regression, Saha and Sarkar (1999) found that the earnings function was nearly flat at primary and high school levels, but shot up with higher secondary and college education. Moreover, when they included informal sector work experience as a separate variable, the rate of return to education dropped to zero, despite formal and informal sector work experience counting for a lot. In short, their study implies that continuing education up to the tenth year will be costly for someone who is unwilling or unable to continue into college. They would be better off terminating school early, starting work in an informal sector, gaining experience and moving to a better paid formal sector job at a later age.

Other earnings studies, such as Bhandari and Bordoloi (2006), Duraisamy (2002), Duraisamy and Duraisamy (1993, 1996) and Dutta (2006) also confirmed that the marginal rate of returns to education were much higher at the college level. Saha and Sensarma (2011) also assessed the rate of returns to academic specialisation. However, these studies mostly considered 1-year cross-section data and may suffer from econometric issues. An important study in this regard was performed by Foster and Rosenzweigh (1996). Using panel data from the Green Revolution, they found that returns to primary schooling significantly increased alongside private investments in education at the time of rapid technical change. Therefore it is misleading to assume that returns to education remained stagnant or very low over a long period of time.

It is also worth emphasising that returns to education are highly tempered by labour-market imperfections, long-term economic policies and job-search frictions. Panel data provide opportunities to control the effects of these intervening factors. Munshi and Rosenzweig (2006) used survey data on school enrolment and income from Mumbai over a 20-year period (1982–2001). They found that lower-caste networks and communities continued to send boys into local language (*Marathi*) schools with the view to channelling them to traditional caste-based (manual work) occupations, while girls were sent to English medium schools to take advantage of the emerging (white-collar) job opportunities in the globalised modern sector. This contrasts with the historical observation that households discriminated against girls when it came to education. The authors argued that in lower-caste communities, girls histori-cally had lower labour-market participation rates and so did not benefit from their caste network; however, globalisation brought about greater returns from the labour market and learning English now paid off.

Traditional institutions (i.e. caste, gender roles and community customs) continue to reinforce past behaviours, which could be inefficient for look-ing at future opportunities. This section concludes by reporting two studies that directly address the issue of dropping out of school.

Pal and Saha (2017a) extended the theoretical model of child labour by Basu and Van (1998) by allowing households to allocate their adult la-bour supply between outside wage employment and self-employment (i.e. a home-based small business). They also considered allocating a child's time between schooling and assisting the parent in their self-employment occu-pation. In this scenario, child labour becomes a substitute for hired labour when the market wage rises. Therefore, in equilibrium, a child's schooling time is likely to fall when market wage rates increase if the household is self-employed. The authors then investigated its empirical possibility using the IHDS 2005 data. The study found that the self-employment status of parents strongly correlated with the hours of work performed by the child; however, the study did not find a positive correlation between wage and child labour.

Shah and Steinberg (2017) took a different approach to the problem of children not being in school. They combined the ASER 2005–09 data on children's education status with the NSS data on the primary activ-ity of household members and rainfall data and found that good rain has opposite effects on schooling depending on the age of the child. For ex-ample, when the child is small, good rain induces better schooling; how-ever, when the child turns into a youth (14–15), a good monsoon leads to an increase in the dropout rate (especially for boys). The authors argued that when a youth reaches an employable age they substitute education for a job in nearby towns or at their parent's work at home, who in turn increase their labour supply to the outside labour market. In summary, the article provides strong evidence of children choosing early employment over education.

These demand-side problems require separate attention, and it appears that the current policy framework is inadequate for addressing these issues. Perhaps the policies towards the informal sector need some rethinking. In addition, how secondary education can be incentivised in direct competi-tion with outside jobs also needs to be explored.

5 NEW EDUCATION POLICY AND CONCLUDING REMARKS

The Government of India is in the process of finalising the New Education Policy after the draft policy underwent a nationwide public consultation. The draft policy document identified 13 themes ranging from learning outcomes and child health to teacher training (Government of India, 2016b). It is heartening to see that the government has put child learning at the top of the agenda. Although the measures that will be taken to improve the learning outcome are not known, the dire learning situation discussed above will hopefully receive serious attention. The second objective that the government aims to pursue is universal secondary education, which seems to be a natural extension of the successful universal primary education. However, this is likely to be extremely challenging due to the presence of both supply- and demand-side issues here. Another objective that may be crucial in attaining the objective of universal secondary education and eliminating the drop-out problem from high school is the incorporation of vocation into secondary education. It is unclear in which form the vocational education could be introduced, whether as a parallel stream or as an integral part of a broader secondary curriculum. This will be vital for encouraging students to stay in high school and acquire valuable skills before going into the job market. Only with 10 years of education, skills and training can the Indian workers be globally competitive.

REFERENCES

ASER, 2016. Annual Status of Education Report (Rural) 2016. Available from: www.aser-centre.org.

Banerjee, A.V., Duflo, E., 2011. Poor Economics: Rethinking Poverty and the Ways to End it. Random House India, Noida, UP.

Banerjee, A., Cole, S., Duflo, E., Linden, L., 2007. Remedying education: evidence from two randomized experiments in India. Q. J. Econ. 122 (3), 1235–1264.

Basu, K., Van, P.H., 1998. The economics of child labor. Am. Econ. Rev. 88, 412–427.

Bhandari, L., Bordoloi, M., 2006. Income differentials and returns to education. Econ. Polit. Wkly. 41 (36), 3893–3900.

Carneiro, P., Ginja, R., 2014. Long-term impacts of compensatory preschool on health and behavior: evidence from head start. Am. Econ. J. Econ. Policy 6 (4), 135–173.

Chaudhary, A.B., Kaul, V., 2015. Ensuring Learning at the Elementary Stage: Are Children School-Ready? I4I E-Symposium. Available from: http://ideasforindia.in/article.aspx?article=Ensuring-learning-at-the-elementary-stage:-Are-children-school-ready?#sthash.4GeYKvDr.dpuf.

Chaudhury, N., Hammer, J., Kremer, M., Muralidharan, K., Rogers, F., 2006. Missing in action: teacher and health worker absence in developing countries. J. Econ. Perspect. 20 (1), 91–116.

Chudgar, A., Quin, E., 2012. Relationship between private schooling and achievement: results from rural and urban India. Econ. Educ. Rev. 31, 376–390.

Currie, J., Thomas, D., 1995. Does head start make a difference? Am. Econ. Rev. 85 (3), 341–365.

Currie, J., Thomas, D., 2000. School quality and the longer-term effects of head start. J. Hum. Resour. 35 (4), 755–774.

Currie, J., Garces, E., Thomas, D., 2002. Longer-term effects of head start. Am. Econ. Rev. 92 (4), 999–1012.

Desai, S., Vanneman, R., 2015. Of Picasso and Cezanne: Early Achievers vs. Late Bloomers, I4I E-Symposium. Available from: http://ideasforindia.in/article.aspx?article=Of-Picasso-and-Cezanne:-Early-achievers-vs.-late-bloomers-#sthash.iM9gYRw5.dpuf.

Desai, S., Dube, A., Vanneman, R., Banerji, R., 2008. Private Schooling in India: A New Educational Landscape. University of Maryland and NCAER.

Duflo, E., Hanna, R., Ryan, S., 2012. Incentives work: getting teachers to come to school. Am. Econ. Rev. 102 (4), 1241–1278.

Duraisamy, P., 2002. Changes in returns to education in India 1983:94: by gender, age cohort and location. Econ. Educ. Rev. 21, 609–622.

Duraisamy, M., Duraisamy, P., 1993. Returns to scientific and technical education in India. Margin, 396–407.

Duraisamy, P., Duraisamy, M., 1996. Sex discrimination in Indian labor markets. Fem. Econ. 2 (2), 41–61.

Dutta, P.V., 2006. Returns to education: new evidence for India, 1983–1999. Educ. Econ. 14 (4), 431–451.

Ed Invest, 2000. Investment Opportunities in Private Education in India. International Finance Organization, Available from: http://www.ifc.org.

Foster, A.D., Rosenzweigh, M., 1996. Technical change and human capital returns and investments: evidence from the Green Revolution. Am. Econ. Rev. 86 (4), 931–953.

Government of India, 2016a. Education Statistics at a Glance. Ministry of Human Resources Development, New Delhi.

Government of India, 2016b. Themes and Questions for Policy Consultation on School Education. Ministry of Human Resource Development. Available from: www.mhrd.gov.in/consultation-theme.

Jimenez, E., Lockheed, M.E., 1991. Private versus public education: an international perspective. Int. J. Educ. Res. 15 (5), 353–497.

Kingdon, G., 1996. The quality and efficiency of private and public education: a case-study of urban India. Oxf. Bull. Econ. Stat. 58 (1), 57–82.

Levitt, S.D., Dubner, S.J., 2005. Freakonomics: A Rogue Economist Explores the Hidden Side of Everything. Allen Lane, New York.

McEwan, P.J., Carnoy, M., 2000. The effectiveness and efficiency of private schools in Chile's voucher system. Educ. Eval. Policy Anal. 22, 213–239.

Munshi, K., Rosenzweig, M., 2006. Traditional institutions meet the modern world: caste, gender, and schooling choice in a globalizing economy. Am. Econ. Rev. 96 (4), 1225–1252.

Muralidharan, K., Sundararaman, V., 2011. Teacher performance pay: experimental evidence from India. J. Polit. Econ. 119 (1), 39–77.

Muralidharan, K., Sundraraman, V., 2015. The aggregate effect of school choice: evidence from a two-stage experiment in India. Q. J. Econ. 130, 1011–1066.

Newhouse, D., Beegle, K., 2006. The effect of school type on academic achievement: evidence from Indonesia. J. Hum. Res. 41, 529–557.

Pal, S., 2010. Public infrastructure, location of private schools and primary school attainment in an emerging economy. Econ. Educ. Rev. 29, 783–794.

Pal, S., Saha, B., 2017a. Parental Self-Employment and Child Labour: Theory and Evidence, Mimeo.

Pal, S., Saha, B., 2017b. Enhancing Excellence: Socially Motivated Schools of Nepal, Mimeo.

Saha, B., Sarkar, S., 1999. Schooling, informal experience and formal sector earnings. Rev. Dev. Econ. 3 (2), 187–199.

Saha, B., Sensarma, R., 2011. Academic specialization and returns to education: evidence from India. J. Educ. Work 24 (5), 501–520.

Shah, M., Steinberg, B.M., 2017. Drought of opportunities: contemporaneous and long-term impacts of rainfall shocks on human capital. J. Polit. Econ. 125 (2), 527–561.

Singh, A., 2015. Private school effects in urban and rural India: panel estimates at primary and secondary school ages. J. Dev. Econ. 113, 16–32.

Somers, M.A., McEwan, P.J., Willms, J.D., 2004. How effective are private schools in Latin America? Comp. Educ. Rev. 48, 48–69.

Tooley, J., Dixon, P., 2003. Private Schools for the Poor: A Case Study from India. CfBT Research and Development, UK.

FURTHER READING

NCERT. 2015. What students of class V know and can do: a summary of India's National Achievement Survey, class V (cycle V). National Council of Educational Research and Training. Available from: www.ncert.nic.in.

CHAPTER 5

Indian Industry: Performance, Problems and Prospects

T.A. Bhavani

Institute of Economic Growth, Delhi, India

1 BACKGROUND

Independent India's development strategy assigned industry the critical role of attaining economic development. Industry was expected to not only produce all the goods hitherto imported (import substitution) to make India self-sufficient but also to absorb surplus labour from agriculture into high productivity jobs and thus place India on a higher path of development. India initiated a wide range of policy measures to attain these objectives. Notwithstanding these government policy initiatives, industry's contribution to the economy in terms of its share in output and employment remained low. The disappointing performance of industry continued even after the economic policy reforms of 1991. Instead, the service sector's contribution to both economic growth and employment generation surpassed that of industry. This prompted some analysts to argue that service-led growth of India was sustainable, although premature given its level of income, understating industry.[a] Other analysts[b] and Indian policymakers believe that industry is still critical for economic development of India and hence needs to be promoted. The government has been trying to revive industry through various policy initiatives over time including the recent 'National Manufacturing Policy' of 2011 and 'Make in India' of 2014.

In this context, this chapter analyses the performance of Indian industry in all its important dimensions by reviewing existing studies.[c] This chapter specifically examines the importance, performance, problems and prospects

[a] For example, see Ghani and Kharas (2010).

[b] For example, Ghose (2016), GOI (1956).

[c] The review is not exhaustive.

of Indian industry. For the purposes of analysis, the paper focuses on industry, particularly the manufacturing sector.[d]

This chapter is organised into five sections. Section 2 briefly discusses the importance of industry in the wider perspective of economic development as well as in the immediate context of India. Section 3 examines the performance of industry in terms of industry and manufacturing shares in gross domestic product (GDP) and employment, their growth rates and productivity and the structure of the small manufacturing segment. Section 4 analyses the factors that are responsible for the slow process of industrialisation in India. Section 5 recapitulates the important findings and makes concluding remarks.

2 THE IMPORTANCE OF INDUSTRY

This section briefly discusses the importance of industry in the wider perspective of development process and structural transformation of any economy, with a specific focus on India.

2.1 Economic Development and Industry

In its simplest form, economic development can be taken as improvements in living standards, which can be attained by satisfying the increasing needs of people through consumption of various goods and services. Society's consumption of goods and services depends on the availability of goods and services and the income levels of people in society. People earn incomes as owners of factors of production, and the income of the majority of the global population is earned by employing their labour services. The main challenge for any economy is having a production structure that maintains the balance between the supply of goods and services (output) and the generation of incomes through absorption of labour (employment generation), which makes it sustainable too. An imbalanced production structure, especially on the employment side, is difficult to manage. Eradicating poverty by enabling every individual to earn enough income to take care of their basic needs is an important and basic component of economic development.

---

[d] Apart from manufacturing, the industry sector also includes mining, quarrying, electricity, gas, and water and construction activities. Of these, manufacturing is the dominant segment, accounting for 68% of the gross output of the industry sector in 2014–15 (statement 1.5, National Accounts Statistics 2016, Central Statistics Office (CSO), Government of India, New Delhi). For the purposes of analysis and arguments, industry and manufacturing are used synonymously. In Section 3, the performances of the industry sector and manufacturing subsector are discussed separately.

To achieve this, the production structure needs to be aligned with factor endowments, especially the labour of the economy.

To elaborate further, production involves transforming factors of production into goods and services. Production units sell their products and share their sales revenues with factors of production (e.g. labour and capital) for their services in the production activity (e.g. wages and salaries provided to labour and returns to capital). Individuals spend their earnings as factor owners to purchase and consume required goods and services. Incomes that individuals earn depend on the production unit's scale of operation and productivity, which further depends on technology and quality of inputs including, labour.

Production activities are classified into three broad categories: agriculture and allied, industry and services, which are also referred to as primary, secondary and tertiary sectors, respectively. The three sectors differ widely in terms of the nature of their operations and products, scale of their operations, technologies, skill requirements, productivities and incomes generated. The production structure (i.e. the combination of all three groups of production activities) that an economy is engaged in, keeps changing depending on factor endowments on the supply side and the level of income on the demand side. The production structure of any economy is closely associated with its level of development.

International experience shows that, in the initial stages of development, the production structure of an economy is dominated by agriculture and the cottage industry due to the primitive technology, unskilled labour and low incomes. With the availability of technological advancements, modern industry slowly arises using surplus labour and income from the agriculture and pushes the economy down the development path through rising incomes and skill improvements. The industry structure itself transforms with the development from labour-intensive to capital and/or resource-intensive to technology-intensive industries over time. As an economy moves further on the development path, modern and productivity-enhancing services (e.g. logistics, finances, information technology and other business services) emerge and complement the growth-enhancing role of manufacturing.[e] This general pattern of structural transformation was first observed by Kuznets and later confirmed by Chenery and others.[f]

In other words, as an economy moves from lower to higher levels of development, industry's contribution rises initially and then falls, exhibiting an inverted U-shaped pattern. The fall in the share of industry is termed

[e] UNIDO (2016).

[f] Dasgupta and Singh (2006) and Ghose (2014).

'deindustrialisation', which occurred at the later stages of development in the currently advanced economies, although one may not be sure of the exact threshold level (range) of income at which deindustrialisation starts in a given country. Technological progress is considered as the main reason for this deindustrialisation.[g] Recent studies indicate that the development process experienced by developing countries broadly follows the same pattern; however, they are reaching the deindustrialisation phase at much lower levels of development possibly because of globalisation and trade. Industry in these countries is taken over by services at much lower levels of income. This phenomenon is referred to as 'premature deindustrialisation'.

Industry and manufacturing are considered vital in the process of development and structural transformation as they can absorb surplus unskilled labour from agriculture into high-productivity and high-income jobs. Kaldor regarded the manufacturing sector as an engine of growth as it is a high-productivity sector compared to the other two sectors. Higher productivity of manufacturing not only leads to its own expansion but also raises the productivity of other sectors through externalities and spill over effects. The income elasticity of demand for manufactured products is also much higher than that for agricultural products.[h] UNIDO (2013) argued that manufacturing, compared to the other sectors, provides a relatively wider employment base with high labour productivity and has a greater possibility to accumulate capital, exploit economies of scale, acquire technology and foster embodied and disembodied technological changes, all of which place the sector at the core of structural transformation. Rodrik (2015) confirmed that manufacturing exhibits strong unconditional convergence in the productivity. Based on cross-country analysis. Felipe et al. (2014) showed that industrialisation, in terms of its employment shares, is a necessary condition for an economy to attain economic prosperity.

2.2 The Indian Context

At the time of independence, India was a low-income, labour-surplus and agricultural economy, where the large majority of labour was unskilled and working in agriculture and allied sectors, which resulted in disguised unemployment and low productivity. This necessitated a shift of surplus labour out of agriculture into high-productivity sectors (i.e. modern industry). In this background, India adopted 'autarkic, public sector-dominated, basic and heavy industry-oriented development strategy', which was implemented in

[g] Rodrik (2015).

[h] Dasgupta and Singh (2006) and Weiss (2011).

a 'socialist pattern of society' framework to attain rapid economic growth along with equity. With a stress on self-sufficiency, Indian policymakers opted for import-substituting industrialisation and started with capital-intensive basic and heavy industry. At the same time, small-scale industries were encouraged to take care of employment generation and equity objectives. The Government of India devised comprehensive policy measures to promote industry and has continued to encourage industry by revising these policies over time.[i]

Notwithstanding policy encouragement, industry's contribution to the economy remained low. Policy efforts continued to boost industry as policymakers believed that industrial development, specifically manufacturing, was essential for India. This was stated explicitly by the renowned economist, Manmohan Singh, who held high positions in economic policymaking and administration, eventually culminating in his reign as Prime Minister of India. During the release of the National Strategy for Manufacturing (2006) by the National Manufacturing Competitiveness Council, he stated that:

> *I do not accept the proposition that India can skip the manufacturing stage of development and can go from being an agrarian society directly becoming services and knowledge-based society. This is a mistaken view. A substantial manufacturing base is essential to absorb the workforce and ensure sustainable growth of the economy .... Indian industry must aspire to be a global player*

The importance of the industry sector for the growth and development of India can be gauged from input flows in the economy. Of the total input requirements of the economy, 60% is provided by the industry sector. Services and agriculture and allied sectors supply approximately 28% and 12% of the total inputs of the economy, respectively. At the sector level, 68% of industry inputs come from itself, 24% come from the services sector and only 8% come from the agriculture and allied sector. Industry also accounts for 45% of service-sector inputs and 21% of agriculture and allied sector inputs. These input shares show the importance of the industry sector in the sustainable growth of India.[j]

---

[i] The major policy initiatives of the Government of India include the Industrial Policy Resolution of 1956, which was initiated alongside the development strategy; Industrial Policy Decisions of 1973 and 1977; Statements on Industrial Policy of 1980 and 1991; National Manufacturing Policy 2011; and the 'Make in India' policy initiative of 2014. In addition, the government time to time initiated numerous sector level policies, including small-manufacturing segment and region-specific policies.

[j] Input–output tables 2007, CSO. Summed up in Box 1.3, p. 7, Economic Survey 2013–14, Ministry of Finance, Government of India.

3 PERFORMANCE

This section analyses, based on the available evidence, the importance of industry, especially the manufacturing sector, in the development process of the Indian economy (in terms of its growth rates, output and employment shares) and its contribution to productivity growth and structural transformation.

3.1 Growth Rates

Decadal averages of annual growth rates (Table 5.1) are used for the analysis in this section.

In the first two decades after independence (i.e. the 1950s and 1960s), the industry sector exhibited, aggregate as well as subsector level, higher average growth rates of output compared to agriculture and service sectors. The average growth rate of the industry sector was 5.74% per annum in the 1950s and 6.45% per annum in the 1960s, whereas the average growth rate of the service sector was 4.18% per annum in the 1950s and 4.88% per annum in the 1960s. The highest average growth rate in the 1950s was experienced by the construction (15.86%) followed by the electricity, gas and water subsector (10.59%). The electricity, gas and water subsector showed the highest average growth rate of 11.38% in the 1960s.

In the 1970s, all the subsectors of industry, except electricity, gas and water, displayed poor average growth rates in the range of 1.95%–4.32%; however, the electricity, gas and water subsector witnessed an average growth rate of 6.93%. The lower growth rates of subsectors brought down the growth rate of industry to 3.69% per annum, which was much lower than that of the services sector (4.46%), and growth of aggregate economy to 2.94%.

The 1980s produced higher growth rates for all the sectors of the economy, including agriculture, pushing up aggregate economic growth by little more than two percentage points. Industry expanded to attain an average growth rate of 6.8% per annum. All the subsectors of industry, except for construction, experienced growth rates of ≥7%, followed by the service sector (6.6%). The growth rates of these two sectors, combined with an exceptional growth of agriculture (4.4%), placed the aggregate economy on a higher growth path, with an average growth rate of 5.8%.

During the 1990s, the industry sector and its subsectors displayed lower growth rates than in the 1980s, with an average of 5.8% per annum for industry and 6% for manufacturing. The growth rate of the service sector

Table 5.1 Average annual growth rate of GDP at constant prices by industry 1950–2010 (%)

Time period	Economy	Agriculture and allied	Industry	Manufacturing	Manufacturing-registered	Mining and quarrying	Electricity, gas and water	Construction	Services
1951–52 to 1959–60	3.59	2.71	5.74	5.61	6.63	4.65	10.59	15.86	4.18
1960–61 to 1969–70	3.96	2.51	6.45	5.89	7.46	6.19	11.38	7.18	4.88
1970–71 to 1979–80	2.94	1.26	3.69	4.32	4.23	3.05	6.93	1.95	4.46
1951–52 to 1979–80	3.5	2.1	5.3	5.3	6.11	4.63	9.63	8.33	4.5
1980–81 to 1989–90	5.8	4.4	6.8	7.0	7.86	8.6	8.99	4.83	6.6
1990–91 to 1999–2000	5.8	3.0	5.8	6.0	6.2	4.9	6.6	5.6	7.6
2000–01 to 2009–10	7.3	2.4	7.3	7.4	7.9	6.8	4.8	9.7	8.9

Source: Data taken from Tendulkar, S.D., Bhavani, T.A. 2012. Understanding Reforms: Post–1991 India. Oxford University Press, New Delhi. Appendix I, Tables A1–A5, pp. 208–210 and Appendix II, Tables 10–1, pp. 231–232.

was much higher (7.6%) than that of all the subsectors of industry. Higher growth of services sector enabled the Indian economy to maintain its growth rate of the 1980s.

The service sector was leading the growth of economy with an average growth rate of 8.91% even in the 2000s. The industry sector displayed an average growth rate of 7.3% per annum with the construction subsector standing out at the top (9.7%) followed by manufacturing (7.4%). Aggregate economy showed an average growth rate of 7.3% per annum in this decade.

In summary, industry was the fastest-growing sector in the Indian economy in the 1950s and 1960s. It was relegated to second position by the service sector in the 1970s, 1990s and 2000s. In the 1980s, industry experienced a growth rate that was marginally higher than that of the service sector. Manufacturing was never the fastest-growing subsector of industry in post-independent India.

3.2 Output and Employment Shares

The analysis in this section is based on Tables 5.2–5.4. Table 5.2 provides decadal average sector shares in GDP at 2004–05 prices since independence. Table 5.3 provides industry shares in GDP for selected countries and Table 5.4 presents the sector composition of employment in India for the specified time points: 1972–73, 1977–78, 1983, 1987–88, 1993–94, 1999–2000, 2004–05, 2009–10, 2011–12.[k]

3.2.1 Output Shares

The contribution of the industry sector and manufacturing subsector to GDP has remained small in the past six decades of independent India. Industry accounted for approximately 27% and manufacturing for 14% of GDP by the end of the 2000s. After reaching 28.22% in 2011–12, the industry share started declining, while the manufacturing share showed signs of decline after reaching 16.28% in the same year.

---

[k] Employment and Unemployment Surveys of the NSSO are the primary source of employment information in India. The NSSO conducts surveys on employment and unemployment covering a large sample of households quinquennially from 27th Round (October 1972–September 1973) onwards. Since then, NSSO carried out nine surveys, the latest being the employment and unemployment survey of the 68th round (July 2011–June 2012). Although the NSSO also carried out surveys on employment before 1972, they were not comparable to the later surveys because of the total departure in procedure and content in 1972–73.

Table 5.2 India: decadal average of sector shares in GDP (%) in constant prices for the period from 1950–51 to 2013–14

Time period	Agriculture and allied	Industry	Manufacturing	Services
1950–51 to 1959–60	50.43	17.50	9.8	29.67
1960–61 to 1969–70	42.93	23.02	12.43	32.51
1970–71 to 1979–80	38.44	24.65	13.67	35.43
1980–81 to 1989–90	32.99	26.22	14.61	40.03
1990–91 to 1990–2000	26.79	24.76	15.28	45.68
2000–01 to 2009–10	18.70	27.81	14.05	53.49
2010–11	14.59	27.92	16.17	57.48
2011–12	14.37	28.22	16.28	57.42
2012–13	13.95	27.27	15.76	58.79
2013–14	13.94	26.13	14.94	59.93

Source: Data taken from Calculations based on yearly shares of the sectors for the period from 1950–51 to 2009–10 given in statisticstimes.com, which mentions its base source as the Planning Commission, Ministry of Planning and Statistics, Government of India, New Delhi.

Table 5.3 Industry and manufacturing share of GDP for selected countries

Country	Manufacturing (%)		Industry (%)	
	2000	2014	2000	2014
India	15	16	26	30
China	32	30	45	43
Indonesia	28	21	46	42
Malaysia	31	23	48	40
Philippines	24	21	34	31
Thailand	29	28	37	37

Source: Data taken from World Development Indicators, World Bank.

In the first five decades of independent India (i.e. up to 2000), industry remained in the third position after agriculture and the service sectors in terms of share of GDP. In the first three decades (1950s to 1970s), agriculture and the allied sector accounted for the largest share in GDP (38%–50%) followed by the service sector (30%–35%). Since 1980, the service sector has been in the lead and it accounted for the largest part of GDP (almost 60%) by 2013–14. Only in the 2000s, Industry became the second largest sector after services in terms of its GDP share. This seems mainly due to the substantial fall in the share of the agriculture and allied sector rather than a significant rise in the industry share.

The industry share in GDP increased by approximately eleven percentage points from 17% in the 1950s to 28% in the 2000s. The rise in the

Table 5.4 India: sector shares (%) in employment for the period from 1972–73 to 2009–10

Time period	Agriculture and allied	Industry	Manufacturing	Services	Non-agricultural
1972–73	73.92	11.30	8.87	14.78	26.08
1977–78	70.98	12.55	10.16	16.47	29.02
1983	68.59	13.78	10.66	17.63	31.41
1987–88	64.87	17.04	12.22	18.09	35.13
1993–94	63.98	14.96	10.63	21.07	36.02
1999–2000	60.32	16.24	11.01	23.43	39.68
2004–05	56.30	18.78	12.27	24.92	43.70
2009–10	51.30	22.02	11.50	26.67	48.70
2011–12	48.90	24.30	12.6	26.90	51.10

a The reference paper calculates these shares based on National Sample Survey Office (NSSO) quinquennial surveys on employment, with the first quinquennial survey being carried out with the reference period of 1972–73 (e.g. the 27th round). This was a marked departure from the earlier employment surveys of NSSO.
Source: Data taken from Papola, T.S., Sahu, P.P., 2012. Growth and Structure of Employment in India. Institute for Studies on Industrial Development, New Delhi, Table 16, p. 36.[a]

industry share was reasonable (approximately 5%) from the 1950s to the 1960s but modest in later decades. This could be due to: (1) the low base share of industry in the 1950s; (2) the industry growth was mostly coming from construction, and electricity, gas and water segments, which constitute a smaller share of this sector; and (3) the lower growth rates of the sector than that of the services sector since the 1970s.

Manufacturing – the largest segment of industry – did not experience enough growth to improve its share substantially. The manufacturing share in GDP increased from approximately 10%–15% over the entire period (1950 – 2010), and most of the increase was seen in the 1960s. Later decades showed modest increase in the manufacturing share of GDP.

Both industry and manufacturing shares of GDP started showing signs of deceleration after reaching their peak in 2011–12. The performance of Indian industry, particularly manufacturing, compares poorly with that of other developing Asian economies including China (Table 5.3). In 2014, China's manufacturing share in GDP was 30%, which was almost double that of the Indian manufacturing share, and its industry share was 70% more than that of the Indian industry.

3.2.2 Employment Shares
The industry sector, which was expected to play a major role in absorbing surplus labour from the low-productivity agriculture and allied sector,

remained in third position after the agriculture and service sectors in employment generation in the economy. The agriculture and allied sector continued to be the major source of employment by employing almost 50 percent of total labour of the economy by the year 2011-12, and the service sector employed another 27% of labour. The industry sector moved closer to the service sector in 2011–12 with a 24% share of employment.

The employment share of the industry sector increased from 11.3% in 1972–73 to 24.30% in 2011–12, while the service sector increased its share from 14.78% to 26 over the same period. The employment share of manufacturing, the major segment of industry, oscillated between 10% and 12% of total employment during 1977–78 to 2011–12.[1] Therefore, one of the objectives of development of industry and manufacturing, of drawing workforce from agriculture and allied activities, remained a distant dream.

Of the total manufacturing employment, around 66% has been generated in the unorganised segment. Of the 34% of employment generated in the organised manufacturing segment, 65% is of an informal nature.[m] Employment in the unorganised manufacturing segment and informal employment essentially means low-income and low-quality jobs that might be little better than agriculture jobs. This is clearly not what independent India's political leadership and the development strategy thought of.

Since 1981, declining trends in Indian manufacturing output and employment have generally been observed, indicating that India has never been adequately industrialised. Indian manufacturing shares in both output and employment reached their peak levels that are far below those of many other developing countries (Amirapu and Subramanian, 2015; Felipe et al., 2014).

As noted in Section 2, the phenomenon of premature deindustrialisation (i.e. the manufacturing sector in developing countries reaching its peak, especially in the case of employment,[n] at a much lower share and level of income than that the developed nations experienced) has generally

---

[1] Note that the employment shares of the manufacturing subsector are smaller than that of its GDP shares.

[m] Srija and Shirke (2014), Table 2, p. 42. Organised manufacturing is broadly defined to include all the enterprises with 10 or more workers. Informal employment is employment without any employment and social security benefits. Enterprise and unit are used synonymously throughout this chapter.

[n] It is the employment than output shares of manufacturing that are more important for the economic prosperity of any nation as employment decides individual incomes and hence welfare.

been observed. For instance, the peak share of manufacturing employment for the world as a whole was attained at 30.5% in 1988 at a per capita GDP level of USD 21,700. However, by 2010 the peak share of global manufacturing employment had fallen to 21% and attained at a level of USD 12,200 per capita GDP. Given these peak global manufacturing shares, and the trends and levels of manufacturing shares in India, Amirapu and Subramanian (2015) referred to Indian industrialisation as 'premature non-industrialisation' and not premature deindustrialisation.

Therefore, does this mean that India should forget industry and manufacturing and pursue a service-oriented development strategy instead? The answer to this question requires further analysis of the sectors in terms of their productivity levels and their contribution to aggregate productivity growth and structural transformation, as the manufacturing sector's importance originated from these factors.

3.3 Contribution to Aggregate Productivity and Structural Transformation[o]

Labour productivity of manufacturing sector was higher than that of the service sector in 1981 and 2010. To be specific, it is the registered (organised) manufacturing segment that displayed high labour productivity but grew at a slower pace than that of services sector. The unregistered (unorganised) manufacturing segment exhibited the lowest productivity at both the time points with the smallest rate of growth (Amirapu and Subramanian, 2015).

Decomposition of aggregate labour productivity growth of the economy for the period of 1981–2011, into (1) sector-specific productivity growth and (2) structural change i.e. the movement of labour from a low-productivity sector to a higher (static reallocation) and faster-growing productivity (dynamic reallocation) sector, revealed that sector-specific productivity growth accounted for a substantial part of growth in aggregate labour productivity. Structural transformation, mainly static reallocation of labour, explained only a small part of aggregate labour productivity growth during the specified time period (Krishna et al., 2017).

Further, productivity growth in the manufacturing and service sector contributed equally to aggregate labour productivity growth followed by agriculture during the initial period of 1981–93. The service sector

[o] Analysis in this subsection is based on two recent studies by Krishna et al. (2017) and Amirapu and Subramanian (2015). Both studies broadly consider the same period (i.e. 1981–2011) although they use different data sources.

productivity growth alone explained most of the aggregate labour productivity growth during 1994–2002, as agriculture productivity growth was stagnant and that of manufacturing declined. The sub period of 2003–11 experienced the highest aggregate labour productivity growth of 7.5%, which was due to growth of labour productivity of almost all the sectors and subsectors of the economy bringing down the relative importance of the service sector (Krishna et al., 2017).

Furthermore, structural transformation during 1981–2011 was limited and happened mainly in the form of static reallocation. Employment generation in the high-productivity manufacturing sector was low. The agriculture sector's contribution to employment remained high although it did decline over time. Job losses in agriculture were largely absorbed in construction, which displayed declining labour productivity, although it remained higher than that of agriculture. Next to construction, it is the service sector, especially trade, transport, storage, financial and business services, hotels and restaurants, that has been absorbing labour (Krishna et al., 2017).

Service subsectors are different from each other in many respects, indicating that the service sector should not be taken as one homogeneous sector. Modern services such as financial services, real estate and business services that are mostly in the organised segment displayed the same traits as that of organised manufacturing. More specifically, modern services displayed higher productivity and enabled the domestic convergence of productivity, but their expansion did not absorb much of resources of the economy (especially unskilled labour) as these are skill-intensive sectors. It is the traditional services (e.g. trade, hotels, restaurants, transport and storage), that operate at lower productivity have been absorbing unskilled labour (Amirapu and Subramanian, 2015).

Traditional services that are mostly produced in the unorganised segment and employ unskilled workers are the most important contributors to service-sector growth. These traditional services account for 58% of total employment and 40% of total output of the service sector (Ghose, 2014). This suggests that service-sector growth in India fits more with the first wave of service-sector growth that comprises more of traditional services and occurs at a lower level of per capita GDP than the second wave of services growth led by modern services that happens at higher levels of per capita income (Eichengreen and Gupta, 2013).

In summary, whether manufacturing or services sector, it is the low-productivity unorganised segment that not only makes significant contribution to output but also generate substantial non-farm employment for unskilled labour. Hence no analysis of these sectors is complete without a discussion of small-scale unorganised segment.

3.4 Small-Scale Industry

Since independence, small-industry segment has been assigned a significant place in the Government of India's plans and policies to tackle employment and equity. For policy purposes, small industrial units are defined in terms of the ceiling limit over investment (purchase value of) in plant and machinery. The ceiling limit was raised over time to account for the price rise in plant and machinery and to enable small units to grow. The latest hike in the ceiling limit was in 2006 to accommodate medium enterprises along with micro and small enterprises. This sector has since been referred to as the micro, small and medium enterprises (MSME) sector[p]; however, this chapter refers to it as the small-scale segment or, sector. Since the sector is defined in terms of investment limits, it overlaps with the organised segment on the upper side and the remaining part falls in the unorganised segment. Further, this sector was originally defined to cover manufacturing enterprises but was later extended to include small-service enterprises in 1985.

The empirical analysis in this section is based on the Fourth All India Census of MSME that was conducted by the Development Commissioner, MSME for the year 2006–07.[q] Although the MSME sector includes both manufacturing and service enterprises, manufacturing constituted 67% of enterprises and accounted for 87%, 88% and 94% of total employment, fixed investment and output of the sector, respectively. Both manufacturing and service subsectors are dominated by microenterprises that contribute substantially to employment. This section focuses on the small manufacturing segment only.

Microenterprises with ≤INR 2.5 million investment in plant and machinery constituted 94% of enterprises, 67% of total employment, 40% of gross output and 33% of fixed investment in the small manufacturing segment. Small enterprises with ≤INR 50 million worth of plant and machinery accounted for 6% of enterprises, 26% of employment, 41% of output and 41% of fixed investment in the small manufacturing segment. Medium enterprises with up to INR 100 million investment in plant and machinery were negligible in number and accounted for only 8%, 19% and

---

[p] The small industrial segment is defined as having three categories, micro, small and medium, with different ceiling limits over investment.

[q] No census has been conducted for later time points.

27% of total employment, output and fixed investment, respectively, in the small manufacturing sector.

One finds wide differences across MSME in terms of scale of operation, capital intensity and labour productivity. Microenterprises were crowded near the lower end and medium enterprises at the upper end of the scale, and small enterprises lying in between in all three parameters. The average medium enterprise was many times larger than a small enterprise irrespective of the criterion considered (i.e. employment, fixed assets or output). They were also highly capital intensive and labour productive. Average small enterprise was much larger and more capital intensive and labour productive than microenterprises.

Further, 96% of small manufacturing units were operating in the unorganised segment by providing employment to <10 workers. These unorganised units contributed around 50% of the sector's employment and fixed assets and approximately 33% of its gross output. Around 25% of enterprises in the small manufacturing sector were reported to have only one employee, presumably the owner.

The main source of technology appeared to be machinery for the majority (87%) of units in the sector as they did not report any explicit source of technology. The majority (90%) of units in the small manufacturing sector accounting for 64%, 56% and 41% of the sector's employment, fixed assets and output, respectively, were proprietary concerns.

In summary, the small manufacturing segment was dominated by tiny proprietary units that are operating at the lower end of the unorganised segment with older technologies and lower productivity; however, this segment continued to be critical for the Indian manufacturing sector as it accounted for a significant part of its output (40%) and employment (66%).

The available evidence presented in this section suggests that industry, especially the manufacturing sector, which was considered as primary instrument of the Indian development strategy, has not performed at the expected level. Industry contribution to both GDP and employment remained small. The manufacturing sector in India is yet to prove that it is a high productivity sector with faster productivity growth, and expanding fast while absorbing labour (specifically unskilled labour). Instead, the Indian manufacturing sector is developed as a sector where the high-capital, and skill-intensive organised segment with higher productivity level coexists with labour-intensive and low-productivity unorganised segment, and growing at a slower pace.

Therefore, questions remain as to why Indian manufacturing did not grow and absorb labour as expected? And how did the unorganised segment, with micro and small enterprises, survive and grow alongside the organised segment for so long? The next section considers the reasons for this Indian phenomenon.

4 FACTORS RESPONSIBLE FOR THE POOR PERFORMANCE OF INDUSTRY

The failure of industry, specifically the manufacturing sector, to expand while absorbing labour is largely due to underlying fallacies and the failure of development strategy and policies.

4.1 Independent India's Development Strategy and Policies

Strong ideological beliefs of independent India's political leadership in economic nationalism and socialism[r] were responsible for India's 'autarkic, public sector-dominated, basic and heavy industry-oriented' development strategy. Policymakers considered international trade as a 'whirlpool of economic imperialism'. To avoid being drawn to it[s] under the influence of economic nationalism, they stressed 'self-sufficiency' and adopted 'import-substituting industrialisation' with an emphasis on basic and heavy industries that made machines to make machines needed for further development.[t] While doing so, policymakers turned a blind eye to the importance of 'self-reliance' and the associated export-promoting industrialisation in then given situation of foreign-exchange crunch.[u] Policymakers rather preferred to manage scarce foreign-exchange resources through state allocation of foreign exchange and import controls.

Policymakers were influenced by the ideology of socialism and stressed 'equity' as one of the primary objectives of the development strategy. Furthermore, with an innocent faith that the state is benevolent and always acts with a social interest, the development strategy assigned a leading role to the state in the industrialisation of the economy. To ensure equitable distribution, state control over industry was deemed necessary through centralised

---

[r] These beliefs were expressed by Jawaharlal Nehru, the first Prime Minister of India, in his book entitled 'The Discovery of India' (Nehru, 1946). These beliefs were shared by society at large.

[s] The Discovery of India, p. 389 (Nehru, 1946). Please note that the page numbers are not uniform across the editions.

[t] The Second Five Year Plan, Chapter 2, para 7 (GOI, 1956).

[u] It was partly due to then existing export pessimism.

investment planning, public sector enterprises (PSEs) and regulations over large private industries. In the process, policymakers disregarded two possibilities: (1) that the state is nothing but a set of politicians and bureaucrats who may pursue their self-interest over social interest, and that political parties may resort to competitive populist policies in the given democratic political set up with universal adult franchise, low incomes and illiteracy and (2) that the state's resources and capabilities may not be adequate to manage the economy and regulate the private sector and markets.

Large private industrialists were equated with war contractors, hoarders and profiteers,[v] and markets were taken to result in inequitable distribution in underdeveloped economies such as India. Therefore, policymakers felt the need to control market transactions and large private industry,[w] totally ignoring the critical role of markets and private industry in alleviating the shortage of goods. At the same time, for equity reasons, the state decided to encourage small-scale private industry through numerous policies.

Thus the development strategy led to a policy set of – (1) stringent controls over foreign exchange and imports; (2) public sector expansion; (3) heavy regulations over large private industry and market transactions and (4) protective and promotional policies for small private industries.

Ideological inclinations and faiths are as such helpful in setting the objectives of development and framing policies; however, the resulting policies should be aligned with the prevalent institutions otherwise policies could be ineffective or counterproductive in the institutional setup. Policymakers did not pay any attention to this aspect.

To channel private investments towards socially-desirable activities, policymakers opted for anticipatory regulations with discretionary and quantitative controls. Anticipatory regulations were designed to prevent any prospective deviation of production activities from social interest rather to punish deviant behaviour on an ex-post basis, without realising that social behaviour cannot be prevented ex-ante as it changes with the institutions (like policies). Discretionary controls, where the implementation of policy controls over industry was at the discretion of concerned officials, required specialised industry knowledge and detailed information about the relevant private industrial units. Even if officials possessed the required information

[v] The Discovery of India, p. 414 (Nehru, 1946).

[w] India had functioning (although limited) markets and private industry at the time of independence. The Constitution of India sanctified private ownership of production means, therefore the government could not wish away private business; and hence opted for controlling it closely.

and knowledge, discretionary regulations always give scope for influencing the officials and thus unproductive rent-seeking activities. Furthermore, policies were designed to control directly economic quantities (i.e. imports and production) instead of regulating them by changing the incentives.

Centralised investment planning and the consequent regulations over the markets and private sector were not aligned with the existing institutional framework of private ownership of production means and their use for private gains in the market environment. This required effective policing of decentralised and dispersed private-production activities, which was physically impossible and prohibitively costly in India. The continuous evaluation of policies with respect to their effectiveness and attainment of objectives is essential to understand the complex interactions between policies and existing institutions. In the case of ineffective implementation or undesirable consequences, policies need to be modified or replaced[x]; however, policymakers neglected this aspect. The following sections discuss the industrial policies of independent India, their implementation and consequences.

4.1.1 Controls Over Foreign Exchange and Imports

Under the import-substituting industrialisation policy, exchange rate was deliberately overvalued in a fixed exchange-rate system to reduce the costs of imports required for development. A variety of restrictions were imposed over imports to contain the resulting excess demand for foreign exchange and to prevent its diversion into non-development purposes. Given the acute shortage of foreign exchange, policymakers went for the direct allocation of foreign exchange among different uses and users through import licenses. The import license allowed a *specified* amount of a *specified* item to be imported by a *specified* user for a *specified* purpose and sometimes even from a *specified* supply source (country). These restrictions were selective in the sense that different ceiling limits were imposed on different items of imports depending on their perceived importance in the development strategy. These controls provided any domestic production activity that was import substituting with complete protection from external competition and thus discouraged exports. Chronic foreign-exchange shortages were inherent in this situation.

The controls over foreign exchange and imports were implemented through case-by-case examination in a complex administrative framework involving multiple departments and agencies. This led to delays and together with changes in quotas and ceiling limits from time to time, resulted in

---

[x] Tendulkar 1993.

dislocation and inflexibilities in production and made it difficult for the industry and economy to respond quickly to shocks. Thus, these controls made industry and economy vulnerable to crises.[y]

4.1.2 Public Sector Expansion

The development strategy recommended that the basic and heavy industry should be in the public sector because of their huge capital requirement and to control the allocation of their output as per social priorities. The Industrial Policy Resolution 1956 (IPR1956) specified the list of industries (17) that were to be developed exclusively in the public sector (schedule A) and the industries (12) that were to be progressively state-owned (schedule B). Until the mid-1960s, public sector expansion occurred mostly in physical infrastructure, iron and steel, and machine-building industries as envisaged in the development strategy. After the mid-1960s, the populist radicalisation of policies by Indira Gandhi resulted in the indiscriminate expansion of the public sector beyond the list of industries specified in the IPR1956 and into non-important private goods production (e.g. bread) and also taking over of sick private units. As a result, the number of central PSEs rose from 84 in 1969 to 246 in 1992.[z]

PSEs were treated as extensions of government welfare departments and used to fulfil multiple and often conflicting objectives, such as the generation of surplus for investment, the generation of employment, the provision of goods and services at subsidised rates, the reduction of regional imbalances disregarding efficiency and commercial viability norms. This was justified in the name of socialism and possible because of soft budget constraint.[aa] As such, PSEs under performed in every respect. Some of the serious problems observed with PSEs were poor project management, lack of technological upgradation, over manning and low-productivity growth.[bb]

Thus the public sector, which was assigned a leading role in the rapid industrialisation of India actually inhibited the performance of industry directly with its inadequate productivity growth and reinvestable surpluses and indirectly by causing the insufficient development of basic and heavy industries and infrastructure facilities.

[y] Joshi and Little (1996).

[z] Handbook of Industrial Policy and Statistics 2008–09 (DIPP, 2009), Table 6.1, p. 151.

[aa] PSEs were said to face a soft budget as they did not go bankrupt despite persistent losses due to government support through budgetary and non-budgetary avenues (Tendulkar and Bhavani, 2012, p. 28).

[bb] Statement on Industrial Policy 1991, para 31.

4.1.3 Private Industry and Market Regulations

Large industry in the private sector was controlled by numerous regulations. The most comprehensive of these regulations was the Industrial Licensing Policy based on the Industries (Development and Regulation) Act (IDRA) of 1951. To channel large-scale private investments to areas of social priority, and to prevent wastage of scarce capital resources through investment in non-priority areas and overcapacity in priority areas, IDRA made government permission compulsory for large private industry[cc] for investment above a specified limit[dd] in specified industries.[ee] An industrial license was necessary to (1) establish a new unit; (2) substantially expand the capacity of a unit in an existing line of manufacturing; (3) carry on the business of an existing unit to which licensing requirements of the Act did not originally apply and (4) change the existing location.[ff]

Furthermore, the entry of large industrial houses[gg] was restricted to only a subset of scheduled industries[hh] to control the concentration of economic power. Large industrial houses were otherwise controlled through the Monopolies and Restrictive Trade Practices Act of 1969. Foreign-owned companies were regulated through the Foreign Exchange Regulation Act (FERA) of 1973 and were only permitted to operate in industries specified in Annexure I of the Industrial Policy (1973) and subjected to specified conditions. The FERA also imposed limits on foreign direct investment.

Technology and factors of production employed in large private industry were also closely regulated. Technology imports had to be approved by the office of the Directorate General of Technology and Development for 'essentiality' and indigenous 'non-availability', which did not permit the import of later technologies. There were also restrictions on capital goods and raw material imports. Large private industry required government permission to raise capital through equity markets under the Capital Issues

[cc] Factories employing ≥50 workers if using power or ≥100 workers if not using power.

[dd] The investment limit was INR 30 million by 1970. Guidelines for Industries 1974–75 (GOI-MID, 1974), pp. 3–4.

[ee] The first schedule of IDRA (1951) specified a list of 42 industries for which the Act would apply; however, this list was enlarged to cover almost all manufacturing activities by the mid-1960s (Bhagawati and Desai, 1970, p. 250; GOI-MID, 1974, pp. 3–4; Marathe, 1986, p. 73)

[ff] Tendulkar and Bhavani (2012), p. 29–30.

[gg] Defined in terms of the floor value of assets of interconnected undertakings initially specified as INR 200 million.

[hh] Industries where planned capacity was falling short of the targets. These industries were specified in Annexure I of the Industrial Policy of 1973.

Control Act of 1947, which controlled both the size and price of the issue. Similarly, both the amount and price of credit were regulated. All aspects of labour employed in large private industry (i.e. hiring and firing, work conditions, wages including social security payment and others) were regulated through multiple legislations. Private industry was also subjected to distribution and price controls, and there were also many industry-specific regulations.

Over time, regulations over large private industry became more detailed and rigorous and were implemented with a case-by-case examination in a complex administrative arrangement that involved numerous departments without any overarching coordination mechanism. All these regulations caused delays and uncertainties, and substantially raised the transaction costs of production activities.

4.1.4 Small Industry Policy

Government commitment to the 'socialistic pattern of society' and the consequent stress on equity required – (i) creation of broad-based employment opportunities and (ii) wide dispersal of industrial production. The small-scale industry was taken to be legitimate instrument for generating employment opportunities and enabling wide dispersal of industrial production.[ii] Small industrial segment was totally left out of government regulations and promoted through a wide range of policy measures.

Small-scale industrial enterprises were, however, perceived to lack competitive strength owing to their limited access to technology and, input and output markets. To protect these units from the competition of large-scale units in the short run, and to improve their access to technology and markets and thus their competitive strength in the long run, government initiated a wide range of policy – protective and promotional, measures.

Protection measures sought to protect small enterprises through a preferential treatment of these over large enterprises. Important protection measures included the reservation of some products for exclusive production in the small-scale sector,[jj] the reservation of products of the small industrial units for purchase preference by government agencies,[kk] input price

[ii] Industrial Policy Resolution 1956. It appears as annexure to chapter 2 of Second Five Year Plan (GOI, 1956).

[jj] The number of products reserved for production in the small-scale industry peaked at over 830 in the mid-1980s.

[kk] The number of small-industry products reserved for government purchase preference were over 400.

concessions (e.g., lower interest rates and electricity tariffs) and numerous fiscal incentives (e.g., excise duty exemption). It may be noted that most of the labour-intensive industrial products, which were having export potential (such as garments and leather), were reserved to be produced in the small manufacturing segment.

Promotional measures sought to improve the competitive strength of small industrial units by improving their access to different markets and through provision of infrastructure, such as developed plots and sheds in industrial estates, consultancy services (economic and technical), industry facilities (like tool rooms and quality testing stations), scarce raw materials, machinery on hire purchase and credit.

Though protection was taken as a secondary objective and protection policies as transitory measures, these were continued, and protection took precedence over the primary and long run objective of improving the competitive strength of the small-scale industry.[l] While continuous protection measures caused the proliferation of small industrial enterprises, including those started by established large industrial companies,[mm] discretionary promotional measures together with lack of information dissemination and cumbersome procedures severely limited the number of enterprises that can avail policy assistance. Thus policy assistance was out of reach for most of the small units. Relatively larger units within the small-scale sector that had better access to policy assistance did not have the incentive to use assistance efficiently and developed a perverse incentive to remain small because of continuous protection coupled with the policy regulations over large private industry. These policies led to a dual structure of this sector with a large number of microenterprises operating at low-productivity levels coexisting with a few large units working at relatively high-productivity levels.

4.1.5 Impact on Industrial Performance

The above-mentioned regulatory policies discouraged productive activities and encouraged unproductive rent-seeking activities. Detailed controls over the large private industry required numerous permissions across several government departments, raising transaction costs, time delays and uncertainties and thus deterred productive activities. At the same time, policy controls, being discretionary, furthered unproductive rent-seeking activities.

[l] Tendulkar and Bhavani (1997) and Expert Committee on Small Scale Enterprises 1997 GOI-DCSSI (1997).

[mm] Goyal et al. (1984) provided numerous examples of the presence of large industrial houses, including multinational corporations, in the small manufacturing sector.

It was generally observed that industrial licenses were obtained by influencing concerned officials through bribes and other means not always to produce but to pre-empt others.

Policy controls constricted the competition by restricting the markets. While industrial licenses and other policies curtailed the domestic competition by creating entry barriers, import controls virtually eliminated any external competition. The limited or lack of market competition did not provide any incentive for producers to improve their efficiency and grow. Detailed policy controls also took away the decision-making power of private producers regarding their production activities. All the basic parameters of production — what to produce (product composition), how much to produce (scale of operation), how to produce (technology) and where to locate and sell, were decided by government officials through industrial licenses. Thus the production units neither had freedom nor incentive to grow through efficient resource utilisation.

Further, factor-price policies, by making scarce capital cheaper and surplus labour resource costly, promoted capital intensive technology and discouraged labour usage in the large private industry. Thus regulatory policies by their very own nature limited the scale of operations, technology upgradation and labour absorption in the industry. It was no wonder that Indian industry was generally observed, in international comparisons, as small and technologically lagging, producing low-quality and high-cost products. By restricting the growth of industry — the primary instrument of the development strategy, regulatory policies resulted in slow growth of the economy and the persistence of market shortages. These consequences were brought out by many academic works and government committees as early as the 1960s and 1970s.[nn] Notwithstanding this feedback, policies were tightened further in the 1970s for political reasons bringing down growth of industry sector as seen in the previous section.

While the policies adversely affected industry/manufacturing sector, they either had a positive impact or did not affect the services in the private sector at all. Although the government had a significant presence in the service sector not only in public administration and defence and social

---

[nn] For instance, the Committee on Prevention of Corruption (also known as the Santhanam Committee) noted the possibility of abuse of discretionary power in the context of scarcity and controls (Myrdal, 1968). The earliest academic studies were of Bhagawati and Desai (1970), Bhagawati and Srinivasan (1976) and Myrdal (1968). Manmohan Singh, the Prime Minister of India from 2004 to 2014, stated that he himself suggested economic liberalisation as far back as 1972 in a paper submitted to the then Prime Minister, Indira Gandhi (Indian Express, Pune, 23 May 2004, op. ed. p. 7).

and community services, but also in the other services such as telecommunications, financial services and education, private sector accounted for a substantial part of the service sector. The nature of services being smaller in size, less visible, less resource (land and capital) intensive, less dependent on infrastructure and logistics and mostly being in the unorganised segment, in comparison with the industry, private sector services did not attract much government attention and were mostly out of its detrimental policies (including tax policies). Industrial policies rather unintendedly benefited the service sector like giving birth to software services. It was the forced exit of International Business Machines (IBM) Company in 1977 due to FERA that gave rise to domestic hardware companies, which had to develop software themselves.[oo] The import of mainframes also forced industry to develop software on their own for its use as well as to export.[pp] The only resource that the service sector required relatively more is labour – skilled as well as unskilled, depending on the nature of the service. Traditional services like wholesale and retail trade, hotels and restaurants, and transport and storage mostly used semi-skilled and unskilled labour whereas modern services like financial services and business services, including software required highly-skilled labour. While unskilled labour is in surplus and available cheaply, independent India's education policy enabled development of skilled manpower through the provision of highly subsidised higher education. All these factors were responsible for sustained and rapid growth of services as against industry.

4.1.6 Policy Reform

The economic situation in 1980 probably compelled Indira Gandhi's government to loosen its earlier radical stance and the resulting policy controls to optimise installed capacities and production, to achieve higher productivity and growth rates of industry.[qq] To this extent, three official committees were constituted to re-examine the regulatory policies.[rr] These committees recommended cautious liberalisation of discretionary controls over investment, capital markets, imports and exports, and limited autonomy to

---

[oo] Soota, 2005 (Balakrishnan, 2006, p. 3868).

[pp] Ramadorai (2011), chapter 2, p. 68.

[qq] Industrial Policy Statement 1980. DIPP (2009).

[rr] The Abid Hussain Committee on import and export policies, the Arjun Sengupta Committee on public sector enterprises and the M. Narashimham Committee on domestic investment, imports and capital issues.

PSEs. Acting on these recommendations, Rajiv Gandhi government that came to power after the demise of Indira Gandhi, undertook deregulation of some of the regulatory policies such as controls over domestic private investment.[ss] While deregulatory measures relaxed supply side constraints on capacity utilisation, rising public spending and higher agriculture growth provided demand stimulus, together they raised the growth of industry and the economy in the 1980s as shown in the previous section. Higher growth in the 1980s, however, was not sustainable due to rising fiscal and external sector deficits and mounting foreign debt. These factors aided by Gulf War in 1990–91 and the resulting hike in oil prices triggered a macroeconomic crisis with a possibility of defaulting foreign debt. In this background, Manmohan Singh, the then Finance Minister in the newly elected Narasimha Rao government, initiated sweeping reforms in 1991 through a paradigm shift in the development strategy toward globalisation, privatisation and liberalisation of the economy in general and industry in particular. The level of reforms can be seen in that the number of mandatory approvals for the private industry was reduced to 421, hardly 5% of the 9227 approvals granted under the IDRA during 1988–91.[tt]

Although economic policy reforms initiated during and after 1991 liberalised private industry from policy controls, these are mostly confined to removing entry barriers to start a business. Numerous operational constraints over industry still remain and dissuade the industry. The Ease of Doing Business 2017 Report of World Bank ranks India, at aggregate level, 130th out of the 190 economies considered. India ranked 185th in dealing with construction permits, 172nd in enforcing contracts and tax payments and 136th in resolving insolvency. The report showed that a construction permit, which is a basic requirement, takes 190 days and costs around 26% of the warehouse value. Another prerequisite to doing business is the ease of enforcing contracts, as business involves a series of contracts with a number of agencies such as vendors and dealers. It takes around 4 years to enforce a contract and costs 40% of claims in India. Indian enterprises pay around 25 taxes that take away 61% of their profits. The implementation of GST will hopefully solve this problem. Although India improved its ranking (136th) in resolving insolvency, it still takes 4.3 years and costs 9% of the estate. The implementation of the Insolvency and Bankruptcy Code (2016) will hopefully make the process easier by reducing the time and costs.

[ss] Tendulkar and Bhavani (2012).

[tt] This study had taken only approvals granted to private industry and did not include mandatory approvals that were rejected (World Bank, 1992).

Another prerequisite for the industrial development of any country is infrastructure facilities such as electricity, ports, roads, transport and tele-communications, which are inadequate and unable to take care of industry requirements in India. In respect of provision of infrastructure, India is lagging significantly behind China and other emerging economies.[uu]

Enforcement of restrictive regulations over labour usage in the organised industry has been in operation since long. Added to it is the enforcement of other regulations such as land acquisition, environment and forest clearances. All these not only deterred private industry directly but also through slowing down of infrastructure development. Consequences of labour regulations over industry have been discussed extensively in the literature. Land acquisition with its rehabilitation and resettlement consequences has become a fertile ground for controversies and an instrument for political parties to win over vote banks and to settle political scores. Acquisition of land by Tata Motors in Singur, West Bengal to produce Nano car with the help of Left government and its forced eviction by Trinamool Congress later is a glaring example in this respect. Though Land Acquisition, Reha-bilitation and Resettlement Act was passed in 2013, it did not make acqui-sition of land for manufacturing easy given its emphasis on the consent of 80% of land owners for private projects and other such provisions, which have been more in favour of land owners. One does not know how much environment and forest clearances are taking care of environment but they definitely stalled government initiated infrastructure projects let alone pri-vate industry. Posco, a Korean steel company, which has obtained approval by the Foreign Investment Promotion Board as early as in 2005, has been struggling to get environment clearances to start its operations in Odisha and about to leave, is a classic example. Policy uncertainty in terms of grant-ing permissions only to abolish them later and retrospective tax provisions is another important factor that frustrates industry. Allocating licenses first through unethical means of lobbying and then abolishing them when there is hue and cry like in the case of 2G spectrum and coal mines does not help. Government has to make sure permissions are granted as per set rules and procedures in the first place.

5 SUMMARY AND CONCLUDING REMARKS

This section recapitulates important findings of the study and provides con-cluding remarks.

[uu] Agrawal (2015) and FICCI and BRIEF (2012).

Independent India's development strategy assigned a critical role to industry as it was considered to be a high productivity sector that can grow faster by absorbing surplus labour from agriculture and lead to growth and structural transformation of the economy. As such, the government initiated numerous policy measures to promote industry. Notwithstanding the policy efforts, the performance of industry in general and manufacturing in particular remained disappointing. Industry was the fastest growing sector in the 1950s and 1960s. It was relegated to second position by the service sector in the 1970s, 1990s and 2000s. In the 1980s, industry showed a marginally higher growth rate than the service sector. Manufacturing – the largest and key component of industry sector – was never the fastest-growing subsector in independent India.

The contribution of industry sector as well as manufacturing to GDP remained small in the last six decades of independent India, with a share of 27% and 16%, respectively, by the end of the 2000s. Their employment shares continued to be much smaller than that of GDP at 24% (industry) and 12% (manufacturing) in 2011–12. Further, most of the manufacturing employment was either generated in the unorganised segment or was of an informal nature, that is, low-income and low-quality jobs. Thus India is still struggling to industrialise despite its policy efforts over the past six decades. One of the objectives of development of drawing surplus labour away from agriculture in to high productivity industry and manufacturing sectors remained a distant dream.

To a large extent, failure of the industry and manufacturing sectors to grow while absorbing labour was due to policy failure. The main factors that were responsible for the dissatisfactory industry performance were: the fallacious assumptions underlying the development strategy regarding the state, international trade, the private industry and markets; the resulting policies of public-sector expansion and anticipatory regulation with discretionary and quantitative controls over foreign exchange, imports and large private industry and protection to small private industry; and the implementation of these policies without paying much attention to their alignment with the existing institutional set-up and evaluation and feedback mechanism. These policies by creating entry barriers and rising transaction costs, time delays and uncertainties, discouraged industrial production activities, and restricted growth, technological upgradation and labour absorption of these activities. Hesitant deregulation in the 1980s and economic policy reforms since 1991 liberalised entry barriers to start a business but numerous operational constraints including regulations over labour, land, environment and forests, infrastructure bottlenecks and policy uncertainties remain, making doing business in India difficult. The industry being highly capital intensive with significant amount of physical capital that is tied up to the production of a specified good and hence cannot easily be shifted to the production of other goods, requires a stable and conducive macroeconomic and policy environment.

Industry is still crucial for the economic development of India, and to develop industry, government has to overhaul its policies. Earlier policies by encouraging unproductive rent-seeking activities developed interest groups both in the government and industry, who continue to exert their influence over policy making and its implementation. Given the democratic political framework, poverty and inequalities, political parties in India have always been for competitive populist policies resulting in uncertain policy environment characterised by short term and piecemeal approach with one step forward and two steps backward. Political parties support one policy and oppose the same policy depending on whether they are with the ruling party or opposition, which itself keeps changing and very few politicians are interested in the content of legislation and its effectiveness in the given situation. Behaviour of parliamentarians over time has gone to extreme levels of either disrupting the parliament sessions or passing legislation without much scrutiny and debate.[vv]

Disruption of parliament sessions causes indefinite time delays in making the required legislations. Passing the legislation without scrutiny affects the quality and hence effectiveness of the legislation and gives scope for litigation. It has generally been observed that Indian society has become more litigious over time. Given the overburdened judiciary system and the consequent inordinate time delays in clearing a case, litigations have severe adverse impact over investments. At the executive level, India is known for its poor implementation. Political masters and bureaucracy have been working more towards protecting their turf or maximising their interests or simply indifferent without paying much attention to immediate institutional requirements for making rules and their implementation[ww] let alone wider interests of the economy.

[vv] For example, the time the Parliament of India spent on discussing the budget reduced from an average of 123 h in the 1950s to 39 h in the last decade (PRS, 2013).

[ww] See the timeline of the FDI policy in the multi-brand retail sector in the previous UPA government.

Only serious actions based on economic realities, replacing rhetoric policy pronouncements, can instil confidence in investors and develop industry. These policies should be holistic and in the wider interest of the economy by balancing the interests of industry with that of others. Fewer regulations that are simpler, rule-based and easy to implement will give less scope for unproductive rent-seeking activities and will encourage productive activities by reducing transactions, time and uncertainties. Complementary policies, not only in physical infrastructure but also in social infrastructure especially in education and skill development, are a must. Education and skill development are of critical importance as industrial development is increasingly driven by labour-saving technological advancements. To start with, government should focus on educating all those segments of population that are out of formal education, especially on their schooling and skill development. Skill development has to be aligned with the job requirements so as to get people jobs immediately. Given the fast changing global economic realities including labour saving technological advancements, India has to move fast in the required directions.

REFERENCES

Agrawal, P., 2015. Infrastructure in India: Challenges and the Way Ahead. Institute of Economic Growth, Delhi, IEG Working Paper No. 350.

Amirapu, A., Subramanian, A., 2015. Manufacturing or Services? An Indian Illustration of a Development Dilemma. Centre for Global Development, Washington, DC, Working Paper No. 409, Available from: www.cgdev.org.

Bhagawati, J.N., Desai, P., 1970. India: Planning for Industrialisation. Oxford University Press, New Delhi.

Bhagawati, J.N., Srinivasan, T.N., 1976. Foreign Trade Regimes in Economic Development, India. Macmillan, New Delhi.

Balakrishnan, P., 2006. Benign neglect or strategic intent. Econ. Polit. Wkly. 41 (36), 3865–3872.

Dasgupta, S., Singh, A., 2006. Manufacturing, Services and Premature Industrialisation in Developing Countries: A Kaldorian Analysis. World Institute for Development Economics Research, UN-WIDER, Helsinki, Research Paper No.2006/49.

DIPP, 2009. Handbook of Industrial Policy and Statistics 2008–09. Department of Industrial Policy and Promotion, Government of India, New Delhi.

Eichengreen, B., Gupta, P., 2013. The two waves of services-sector growth. Oxf. Econ. Pap. 65, 96–123.

Felipe, J, Mehta, A., Rhee, C., 2014. Manufacturing Matters: But It's the Jobs That Count. Asian Development Bank, Manila, ADB Economics Working Paper Series No. 420.

FICCI and BRIEF, 2012. Lack of Affordable & Quality Power: Shackling India's Growth Story. Federation of Indian Chambers of Commerce and Industry; Bureau of Research on Industry and Economic Fundamentals, New Delhi.

Ghani, E., Kharas, H., 2010. 'The Service Revolution', Economic Premise, No.14 (May), Poverty Reduction and Economic Management (PREM) Network. The World Bank, Washington, DC.

Ghose, A.K., 2014. India's Services-Led Growth. Institute for Human Development, New Delhi, Working Paper No. 01, Available at: www.ihdindia.org..

Ghose, A.K., 2016. India Needs Rapid Manufacturing-Led Growth. Institute for Human Development, New Delhi, Working Paper No. 01, Available from: www.ihdindia.org.

Goyal, S.K.K.S., Rao, C., Kumar, N., 1984. Small Scale Sector and Big Business. The Indian Institute of Public Administration, New Delhi.

GOI, 1956. Second Five Year Plan. Planning Commission, New Delhi.

GOI-MID, 1974. Guidelines for Industries 1974–75. Ministry of Industrial Development, Government of India, New Delhi.

Joshi, V., Little, I.M.D., 1996. India's Economic Reforms. Oxford University Press, New Delhi.

Krishna, K.L., Erumban, A.A., Das, D.K., Aggarwal, S., Das, P.C., 2017. Industry Origins of Economic Growth and Structural Change in India. Centre for Development Economics, Delhi School of Economics, Delhi, Working Paper No. 273, Available from: www.cdedse.org.

Marathe, S.S., 1986. Regulation and Development: India's Policy Experience of Controls over Industry. Sage, New Delhi.

Myrdal, G., 1968. Asian Drama: An Inquiry Into the Poverty of Nationsvol. 2Allan Lane, The Penguin Press, New York.

Nehru, J., 1946. The Discovery of India. The John Day Company, New York.

Papola, T.S., Sahu, P.P., 2012. Growth and Structure of Employment in India. Institute for Studies on Industrial Development, New Delhi.

PRS, 2013. Rethinking the Functioning of the Indian Parliament: Background Note for the Conference on Effective Legislatures. PRS Legislative Research, New Delhi, Available from: www.prsindia.org.

Ramadorai, S., 2011. The TCS Story & Beyond. Portfolio, Penguin, India.

Rodrik, D., 2015. Premature Deindustrialisation. National Bureau of Economic Research (NBER), Cambridge, MA, NBER Working Paper Series No. 20935.

Srija, A., Shirke, S.V., 2014. An Analysis of the Informal Labour Market in India: Economy Matters. Confederation of Indian Industry (CII), New Delhi, September–October 2014, pp. 40–46.

Tendulkar, S.D., 1993. Institutional environment and regulatory regime. In: Ahuja, K., Coppens, H., van de Wustern, H. (Eds.), Regime Transformation and Global Realignments: Indo-European Dialogues on the Post-Cold War World. Sage, New Delhi, pp. 279–294.

Tendulkar, S.D., Bhavani, T.A., 2012. Understanding Reforms: Post-1991 India. Oxford University Press, New Delhi.

Tendulkar, S.D., Bhavani, T.A., 1997. Policy on modern small scale industries: a case of government failure. Indian Econ. Rev. 32 (1), 85–110.

Weiss, J., 2011. The Economics of Industrial Development. Routledge, London.

World Bank, 1992. India: Stabilising and Reforming Economy. Country Operations, Industry and Finance Division, India Country Department, South Asia Region, Report No. 10489 (18 May 1992).

World Bank, 2017. Doing Business 2017, Economy Profile 2017, India. World Bank, Washington, DC, Available from: www.doingbusiness.org.

UNIDO, 2013. Sustaining Employment Growth: The Role of Manufacturing and Structural Change, Industrial Development Report 2013. United Nations Industrial Development Organisation, Vienna.

UNIDO, 2016. The Role of Technology and Innovation in Inclusive and Sustainable Industrial Development, Industrial Development Report 2016. United Nations Industrial Development Organisation, Vienna.

FURTHER READING

Bhavani, T.A., 2016. Structure of the Indian small scale-sector in the post-reform period: a case of policy failure. In: Veeramani, C., Nagaraj, R. (Eds.), International Trade and Industrial Developments in India: Emerging Trends, Patterns and Issues. Orient Blackswan, Hyderabad, pp. 172–201, Chapter 7.

GOI-DCSSI, 1997. Report of the Expert Committee on Small Enterprises. Department of Small Scale, Agro and Related Industries, Government of India, New Delhi.

GOI-DCMSME, 2008. All India Census of Micro, Small and Medium Enterprises: Final Report. Ministry of Micro, Small and Medium Enterprises, Government of India, New Delhi.

GOI-MOF, 2014. Economic survey 2013–14, vol.1. Ministry of Finance, Government of India, New Delhi.

GOI-MOF, 2015. Economic Survey 2014–15, vol.1. Ministry of Finance, Government of India, New Delhi.

Kochhar, K., Kumar, U., Rajan, R., Subramanian, A., Tokatlidis, I., 2006. India's Pattern of Development: What Happened, What Follows? International Monetary Fund, Washington, DC, IMF Working Paper No. WP/06/22.

Mohan, R., 1992. Industrial policy and controls. In: Jalan, B. (Ed.), The Indian Economy: Problems and Prospects. Vikings, New Delhi, pp. 85–115.

Mohan, R., Aggarwal, V., 1990. Commands and controls: planning for Indian industrial development, 1951–1990. J. Compar. Econ. 14, 681–712.

Rakshit, M., 2007. Services-led growth: the India experience. Money and Finance, 91–123.

Rangarajan, C., Seema, E., Vibeesh, M., 2014. Developments in the workforce between 2009–10 and 2011–12. Econ. Polit. Wkly 49 (23), 117–121.

Rowthorn, R., Ramaswamy, R., 1997. Deindustrialisation: Its Causes and Implications. International Monetary Fund (IMF), Washington, DC, Economic Issues 10.

Srinivasan, T.N., 1991. Reform of industrial and trade policies. Econ. Polit. Wkly. 26 (37), 2143–2145.

CHAPTER 6

Civil Society Matters: India in Continuity

Rama P. Kanungo

Newcastle University London, London, United Kingdom

1 INTRODUCTION

Civil society is all-embracing when the purpose of governance and stewardship is concerned. Dating back to Aristotelian times, it has evolved and emerged as the cornerstone of modern democratic institutions.[a] Civil society refers to the commitment, accountability and inclusivity of common man in the process of building a harmonious society. No authority alone bears the onus of general welfare and development in this kind of society, but rather it is shared. Thinkers from 18th century Europe perceived that an all-purpose absolute form of state or authority could pose a threat to civil society in its wider form. Therefore, they raised issues surrounding social realism versus the common man's society.

The state should maintain the right balance between the governance of state and the functions of civil society so that all people receive societal benefits and can support the state. The theory of a prominent civil society has had a profound impact on the general democratisation theory, which has led to liberalism and the social partisan view. Nevertheless, many theorists find that the modern concept of civil society suffers from its inherent western biases and lacks global relevance.

The contemporary debate surrounding the state versus civil society suggests that the existence of a powerful state is a pre-condition to sustaining a civil society. A well-functioning civil society requires support from the state and can create a harmonious togetherness among its people. However, the overpowering concept of state began to emerge at the beginning of the

[a] See Berglund, H., 2009. Civil Society in India: Democratic Space or the Extension of Elite Domination? Working Paper 2009:1, Stockholm University. Cross-reference to Keane, J. (ed.), Civil Society and the State: New European Perspectives, Verso: London, 1988; Hall, J.A. (ed.), Civil Society: Theory, History, Comparison, Polity Press: Oxford, 1995; and Cohen, J.L. and Arato A., Civil Society and Political Theory, MIT Press: Cambridge, MA and London, England, 1992 for introductions to the historical development of the concept.

Changing the Indian Economy
http://dx.doi.org/10.1016/B978-0-08-102005-0.00006-X
109

18th century, whereas the role and representation of civil society became marginal.

2 CIVIL SOCIETY: AN ACCOUNT

The socio–political system of India generally differs from that of the western world. The formation of civil society in India exhibits numerous commonalities and, at times, sharp contrasts with the western world. Many western states have simultaneously developed alongside civil society over the centuries through an emerging process and have maintained an incremental shift towards a powerful and efficient state. At the same time, most western states have progressed towards a more independent and open civil society. The emergence of civil society in India has not been as consistent, except for in the Vedic and post–Vedic periods when localised democratisation prevailed. Both pre-colonial and colonial states reigned absolute when the state coexisted with powerful and influential religious outfits and traditional power structures. The remit of state reached far outside of the social realism and defied the alternative power system. The Indian practice of having native religious elites and overpowering religious identity proliferated state hegemony, whereas civil society played a minor role (Ali, 2001). The 19th century socio-religious movement in India made radical changes to the wider social context and reformed many traditional beliefs and faiths; however, the freedom movement meant that several changes were overshadowed by the spread of foreign influence and fierce nationalism.

Many of the social trends strengthened the freedom movement and implicitly contributed to the formation of civil society. During the early 20th century, the national resistance movement, led by the Indian National Congress, became the driving force for social renewal and the primary source for modern India's civil society. The social activism surrounding the independence movement was mainly anticolonial and aimed at producing a free sovereign state. The idea of civil society was secondary in the movement. Many other significant forms of social movement gained momentum during that period, including women's participation, labour reorganisation, revenue settlements, classification of civil and criminal jurisprudence and educational reforms. For example, the All Indian Trade Union Congress was formed in 1920, the language of education became increasingly English and land and revenue coding began. In addition, the penal code was implemented, and the reduction of provincial authority took place irrespective of the anticolonial temperament of the people. Despite wider reforms being initiated, the national bourgeoisie and middle-class political activists remained loyal to the state and the progressive classes could not influence the common man in society. After independence was won and the colonial princely states were dismantled, the state-dominated economy remained prevalent in India. The government promoted central planning with a non-federal approach, in which the role of civil society was not taken seriously and civil society's collective contribution was not recognised. Post-independence civil society took a considerable time to restructure and adapt to the new governance regime. During the 1960s and 1970s, India faced several natural disasters and wars; however, both rural and urban Indians continued their attempt for a better civil society through a process of social renewal via declassification and destratification. Such changes, primarily aimed at addressing the material and social needs of the population, were mainly attached to the wider ideological movements challenging the conventional outlook of society. In mid-1975, India declared a national emergency which remained until the 1977 election. The declaration of a national emergency curtailed most of the democratic processes, breached parliamentary federalism and led to severely limited civil rights. The enforcement of this national emergency spiralled into a civil disobedience movement that was seen during the British Raj and spawned neosocial movements and numerous liberal social groups. Environmental issues, women's emancipation, girl-child protection, managed family planning and gender identity became the mainstay of the civil movement during this time. This was a transitional phase in which India witnessed changes that reshaped traditional socio-cultural perceptions. Along with reforming the democratic and progressive state, civil society learnt to claim its rights and contest injustice. Beginning in the 1980s, the state encouraged participation in civil movements to achieve a lateral shift in social development. Collective and organised public initiatives were undertaken to establish a liberal alignment with global trends. The International Monetary Fund (IMF) and the World Bank were keen to facilitate capital and labour flow across the continents by means of foreign direct investment, which resulted in infrastructure development and socio-economic mobility.

Over the years, Indian civil society has suffered from many inequalities due to socio-economic, ethnic and religious disparities. The principles and practices of equality, commitment and accountability have not been fully experienced within the wider Indian society. In addition, large segments of the Indian public are excluded from the core stream of society and inherently biased towards caste, class and religious preferences. The segmentation of social layers has undermined the strength of civil society, and societal non-cohesiveness continues with elitism in different identities and shapes, where apathetic sentiment and surficial mobilisation are seen within civil society engagement. The liberal civil society movement has gained momentum in recent years; however, many contravening elements (i.e. confrontational and ideological nationalism) have impeded progress. This reflects a classic scenario of the struggle of civil society, where success cannot be defined by class interest and economic growth. The hubris of ideology and nationalism must not undermine secular Indian democracy, where inclusiveness and parity should be equitable among different sections of society. No civil society would be able to thrive with exclusive and parochial perspectives.

3 CIVIL SOCIETY AND REFORMS: A REMAKING

Civil society in India is currently gaining momentum and becoming more prominent than ever before; however, the core virtues and principles of Indian civil society trace back to the concept of 'Dharma'. Dharma, in the Hindu belief system, denotes the common good for the people and upholding the practices of karma, which represents proactive engagement for the collective betterment.

Nevertheless, the noble tenets eroded over time and medieval Indian society plunged into the strife of caste, religion and hierarchy elitism. The advent of liberal thoughts that are central to a civil society (i.e. liberty, equality and fraternity) only emerged through reformist Indians and westerners and challenged the orthodox beliefs. Social disparities, conventional inequality and discriminatory hierarchy were progressively shunned by the advancing neo-liberalism as a countermeasure to confront key social inertia. A reformist civil society began to emerge which mobilised the sense of common people towards a more unprejudiced and sharing society. Pre-independence social movements, including civil disobedience, satyagraha and non-cooperation under Mahatma Gandhi's stewardship, inspired people to seek social renewal. The common man became a part of wider social institutions and was empowered to participate in public systems beyond political affiliations; however, the reality of achieving a clearly inclusive and sustainable civil society is far away and has not yet become a reality despite many reforms. Movements for social changes in India have always been sporadic and isolated, although a few nationwide movements were seen in recent decades. Pre- and post-modern Indian society never characterised the contemporary form of self-constitution and civic morality. Therefore the progressive role of civil society in rationalising the reforms was never clearly understood by the common people of India. The egalitarian and democratic norms of Indian civil society began to emerge as India opened to new world order after independence. India has evolved since independence, and the identity of civil society as a consequence of wider social reform has become more acceptable. The liberal economic approach of the IMF, World Bank and European Monetary Fund triggered economic changes that have affected many countries, including India. Public initiatives and engagement in the socio-economic system without institutional state ownership developed as a general trend in India. The state being the only developmental provider became increasingly irrelevant, and people sourced socio-economic benefits from non-governmental agencies and organisations.

The experience from the colonial legacy continues to date and has led to class divisions and caste separation among Indians. Despite many changes throughout the years, the exclusivist identities of social strata remain among the different social tiers within Indian society. The relative failure of the Indian state to engage people in participating in socio-economic spheres has created exclusion and segmentation, which are biased towards the class and caste interests (Berglund, 2009). However, Indian society has made some progress in eradicating such disparities through societal organisations [i.e. non-governmental organisations (NGOs)]. Although it is generally accepted that the government is primarily responsible for socio-economic developments, relying solely on governmental initiatives will not suffice. Therefore NGOs now play increasingly significant roles in the development of a more stable civil society in India. Sharan produced a typology of civil society organisations in India (Singh, 2012) that included:

1. Gandhian-influenced voluntary groups (their number has fallen)
2. Rural development agencies run by professionals, corporations and smaller groups
3. Civil and political rights groups
4. Missionary organisations (i.e. Christian Mission and R.K. Mission)
5. Student, worker and women's movements related to the left and other political parties
6. Independent social movements (i.e. Dalits, Adivasis, women and environmentalists)
7. Minority movements and groups (i.e. Muslim, Christian, Buddhist etc.)
8. Religious movements (both spiritual and fundamentalist)

Social outfits (i.e. NGOs and other civil society organisations) are becoming key players in the political, social and economic areas of India. Their contributions add value to the state structure by improving the governance and transforming the state. The movement to maintain a stronger civil society in India is gaining momentum; however, the relationship between civil society and the common people in India is somewhat intermittent and sporadic. Reinforcing the connection between civil society and the people can be achieved by establishing a responsive government and a supportive bureaucratic system. Equitable resource allocation via policy implementation is also equally important for such engagements. Moreover, India needs transparent, participatory and accountable governance along with a fair judiciary system to eventuate the role of civil society in the building of a robust state. Several governmental, administrative and judiciary functions need reforming to align the role of civil society with people's aspirations. The following areas require attention:

1. Accountability and Transparency: A sense of outward responsibilities should be developed, and the government, as state, should be accountable for providing openness and transparency in its conduct. Beyond political citizenship, a more societal citizenship is also required to create transparency in India. A sense of belongingness and equality are essential for the collective good and can be achieved through civil society mobilisation. Transparency International reports[b]

   "India's ongoing poor performance with a score of 40 reiterates the state's inability to effectively deal with petty corruption as well as large-scale corruption scandals. The impact of corruption on poverty, illiteracy and police brutality shows that not only the economy is growing – but also inequality".

2. Renewal of Education: The extant education system is multi-layered and needs to be more streamlined to meet the demands of the global workforce. In addition, the level of primary and secondary education is also staggeringly low compared with the total population (Tables 6.1 and 6.2).

Table 6.1 Population census (2001 and 2011)

	2001	2011
Total	102.87	121.06
Male	53.22	62.31
Female	49.65	58.75

Source: Office of the Registrar General and Census Commissioner, India (http://censusindia.gov.in/).

[b] http://www.ey.com/Publication/vwLUAssets/EY-Transparency-International-Corruption-Perceptions-Index-2016/$FILE/EY-Transparency-International-Corruption-Perceptions-Index-2016.pdf

Table 6.2 Estimated population in 2013 and 2014 by age group

Age (years)	2013			2014			Corresponding level of education	2012		
	All	SC	ST	All	SC	ST		Male	Female	Total
6–10	130,896	23,324	13,020	130,648	23,286	12,971	Primary (I–V)	68,583,442	62,560,241	131,143,683
11–13	75,223	13,259	7,194	74,413	13,127	7,079	Upper primary (VI–VIII)	39,946,948	36,097,179	76,044,127
6–13	206,119	36,583	20,214	205,061	36,413	20,050	Elementary (I–VIII)	108,530,390	98,657,420	207,187,810
14–15	50,244	8,803	4,610	49,801	8,724	4,559	Secondary (IX–X)	26,706,389	23,984,866	50,691,255
6–15	256,363	45,386	24,824	254,862	45,137	24,609	I–X	135,236,779	122,642,286	257,879,065
16–17	45,085	7,749	3,963	44,734	7,680	3,937	Senior secondary (XI–XII)	24,139,427	21,299,011	45,438,438
6–17	301,448	53,135	28,787	299,596	52,817	28,546	I–XII	50,845,816	45,283,877	96,129,693
18–23	140,802	24,077	11,926	141,046	24,106	11,949	Higher education	73,294,003	67,264,696	140,558,699

Source: Ministry of Human Resource Development, Government of India (http://mhrd.gov.in/statist) www.censusindia.gov.in/Census_Data_2001/India_at_glance/Popul.aspx.

3. Collective Policy-making: Different levels of policy-making departments should participate in policy dialogues, and key stakeholders should be considered via public consultation. The process should include the three different tiers of the government: local, provincial and central. All internal and external stakeholders must remain informed to avoid any information asymmetry, and the right to information should be prioritised.

4. Employment and Underemployment: One of the key factors that limit employment growth is underemployment (i.e. the availability of a skilled workforce but the absence of employment opportunities). To tackle this issue, the government should consider employment allocation which is commensurate with available skilled personnel through sensitisation of the people through civil society engagement.

5. Environmental Awareness: Managing environmental issues and abiding by the international agenda are key necessities for the government. These issues can be managed through the multi-lateral engagement of NGOs. The key issues include population growth, air pollution, loss of biodiversity, land and soil degradation, deforestation, carbon emissions, water pollution and garbage disposal. According to the McKinsey Global Institute,[c] India will have more than 68 cities with populations greater than 1 million by 2030, and over 40% of Indians will live in cities with more than 1 million people by 2025.[d]

6. Elementary Institution Building: The government should create sufficient awareness of the socio-political process, starting from the basic necessities of villages and panchayats. Thus rather than being solely representative, the role of civil society as a constituent of a participatory democracy can be strengthened and lead to a stronger local government. The government has undertaken a number of initiatives in recent years;[e]

[c] https://www.mckinsey.com/mgi/overview
[d] https://www.azocleantech.com/article.aspx?ArticleID(551
[e] https://www.indiastat.com/administrativesetup/1/panchayats/200/stats.aspx. Statewise funds sanctioned/released and expenditure incurred under Rajiv Gandhi Panchayati Sashaktikaran Abhiyan (RGPSA)/Rashtriya Gram Sawaraj Abhiyan in India (2012–13 to 2017–18, upto 24 July 2017). Sectorwise village development plan progress report under Saansad Adarsh Gram Yojana (SAGY) in India (as on 31 January 2017). Selected statewise number of skill development projects from village development plans of SAGY Gram Panchayats in India (as on 27 July2017). Statewise allocation and release of grants to local bodies for Panchayati Raj Institutions by the 14th Finance Commission in India (2015–16 and 2016–17). Statewise funds sanctioned for E-enablement under RGPSA in India (2012–13 to 2016–17). Statewise number of Gram Panchayats (GPs) planned to be made Nirmal Grams in India (2012–17). Statewise status of adoption of SAGYGPsprojects (phaseII) in India (as on 27. January 2017).

however, the involvement of civil society organisations in this process has been limited.

7. Social Justice for Health: A comprehensive healthcare system is paramount for inclusive governance and social well-being. The Indian government initiated an integrated healthcare policy in 2017 which stated that:

"The main objective of the National Health Policy 2017 is to achieve the highest possible level of good health and well-being, through a preventive and promotive healthcare orientation in all developmental policies, and to achieve universal access to good quality healthcare services without anyone having to face financial hardship as a consequence".[f]

The draft policy proposed in 2015, the National Health Rights Act, aims to increase the allocation of GDP for healthcare by 2.5% and is an alternative to universal health care, which offered healthcare as a fundamental right.[g] Hence the primary goal of healthcare as a fundamental right for all remains unreachable. In a report published in 2015, Deloitte stated that:

"however, challenges remain. The vision for the plan period of 2012–17 is to achieve acceptable standards of health care for the Indian populace. However, India still does not have a central regulatory authority for its healthcare sector".[h]

8. Human Rights and Vigilance: Without a robust human rights framework, the process of democratisation remains incomplete. The accountability of the government to balance governance with human rights is key to the functioning of a liberal civil society. Extra judicial activities, violations of human rights and administration aberrations have occurred over the years in India. A report by the Human Rights Data Analysis Group and Ensaaf presented verifiable and quantitative findings that showed that human rights are largely violated in India.[i] Institutional reform and the empowerment of civil society are central to the implementation of human rights. The Human Rights Watch published a report in 2016 entitled 'Events India 2016', which questioned the government's role. The report[j] stated that:

"The Modi government continues to use the Foreign Contribution Regulation Act (FCRA), which regulates foreign funding for civil society organizations, to cut

---

[f] http://pib.nic.in/newsite/PrintRelease.aspx?relid(159376

[g] http://indianexpress.com/article/what-is/what-is-national-health-policy-2017-4574585/

[h] https://www2.deloitte.com/content/dam/Deloitte/global/Documents/Life-Sciences-Health-Care/gx-lshc-2015-health-care-outlook-india.pdf

[i] https://hrdag.org/india/

[j] https://www.hrw.org/world-report/2017/country-chapters/india#33ae4d

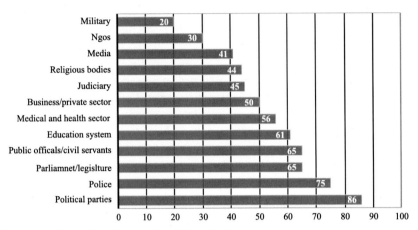

Figure 6.1 *Perception of corruption by institutions.*

off funds and stymie the activities of organizations that question or criticize the government or its policies. In April 2016, Maina Kiai, the UN special rapporteur on freedom of assembly and association, analysed the FCRA and said that restrictions imposed by the law and its rules "are not in conformity with international law, principles and standards".

9. Eliminating Corruption: Corruption is rampant in India. Transparency International found India to be the most corrupt country in the Asia-Pacific region with a 69% bribery rate across public sectors.[k] Fig. 6.1 is based on Transparency International data and indicates the different levels of corruption among various Indian sectors. The threat of corruption has been an overarching issue over the last 50 years, and civil society organisations have made innumerable attempts to moderate it; however, morals and ethics play a crucial role in the fight against corruption and they can be encouraged among common people via civil society engagement.

10. Harmony of Religious and Faith System: India has long suffered from religious elitism and conflicting faith systems. The sheer volume of diverse religious beliefs and practices makes India unique. India maintains constitutional secularism under the 42nd amendment in 1976. The post-colonial period witnessed numerous violent incidents and civil agitations due to religious and sectarian strife, and religious frictions remain to this day. The Los Angeles Times reports that religious tension could potentially damage reform initiated by the current government.[l]

[k] http://www.businesstoday.in/current/economy-politics/india-most-corrupt-country-in-asia-corruption-rampant-in-education-healthcare-forbes/story/259512.html

[l] http://www.latimes.com/world/asia/la-fg-india-religious-tension-reforms-20151030-story.html

4 GOVERNANCE AND POLICY: CIVIL SOCIETY ORGANISATIONS

The process of governance in India is representative rather than partici-patory. There is always a separation between governmental outfits and the common man. Therefore people have limited chance to voice their concerns to government representatives, except through civil society bod-ies; however, Indian people have associated them with socio-political and cultural pluralism but have never consciously understood how the pro-cess of governance and grievance works and what their entitlements are. Society is currently becoming more aware of the civil space and their entitlements. Policy-making and administration are two key tools for par-simonious governance in democratic states. Civil society organisations primarily serve the public in sub-systems and help the government with policy-making and administration. Civil society manifests the aspirations of the people via institutional reform, entitlements and on-going gov-ernance of the state. Renukumar (The Centre for Good Governance, India)[m] outlined the functions of governance and its interrelatedness with other state institutions.[n]

Indian civil society has begun to have an influential effect on the state of governance and policy-making through institutional affiliations. India is the second most populous country in the world but has a dismal Gini coefficient (i.e. 33.9% for 2013), which clearly indicates that inequality in income is pervasive.[o] Such disparity in the post-liberalised Indian society creates social distress and class friction, which leads to disengagement and factionalism. The role of civil society in addressing issues such as inequality is becoming far more important than before. This goal can only be achieved through robust policy-making via multi-lateral dialogue between civil so-ciety organisations and the government. Effective policies and governance should converge to deliver the desired benefits to society through dedicated civil society undertakings.

[m] https://cgg.gov.in

[n] Good Governance: Concepts and Components. Available from: https://www.slideshare.net/nayanarenu/good-governance-6268274

[o] A measure of the deviation of the distribution of income among individuals or households within a country from a perfectly equal distribution. A value of 0 represents absolute equal-ity, whereas a value of 100 indicates absolute inequality (http://hdr.undp.org/en/content/income-gini-coefficient). Sourced from: World Bank, 2013. World Development Indicators 2013. Washington, DC.: World Bank. Available from: http://data.worldbank.org. Accessed in October 2013.

Seven key areas for inclusive and effective governance through policy-making can be delivered in consultation with civil society organisations.

4.1 Governance Through Participatory Policy-making

Civil society, along with the government, can create a robust policy framework. The interdependence and wider functionality between the government and civil society are central to achieving successful governance. However, at times, civil society can be the most vociferous critic of the government. Contrary to the government's contributions, civil society often supports and leads many societal causes that fundamentally differ from the welfare purpose of the public. Civil society constitutes a collection of organisations affiliated through representation and inclusivity; however, the government is not always capable of maintaining this same level of involvement due to diverse political agendas, choices and rationales. The United Nations Economic and Social Council explains participatory governance as:[p]

"Governance entails processes and institutions that contribute to public decision-making. When those processes and institutions concern the public sector, the term public governance is used. It can be argued that there are three categories of public governance: civic, political and development. Civic and political governance deal with issues that are related to human rights. Development governance mainly pertains to planning, budgeting, monitoring and accountability of socio-economic development policies and programmes. Participatory governance is one of many institutional strategies of development governance. Citizen engagement is the desired outcome or logical end of participatory governance"

Civil society organisations can implement participatory governance through citizen engagement. To achieve this, the government should involve civil society organisations at primary, secondary and tertiary levels of policy-making. Other countries now engage civil society organisations in public accountability processes including audits.[q] India is increasingly embracing civil society engagement; for example, the Citizen's Report Card System, which is a citizen-based monitoring and public accountability system at the local government level, has been created. However, India needs a

[p] http://unpan1.un.org/intradoc/groups/public/documents/un/unpan025375.pdf

[q] 'Auditing for Social Change', Department of Economic and Social Affairs, 2007 (ST/ESA/PAD/SER.E/75); 'Dialogue on Civil Society Engagement in Public Accountability', Department of Economic and Social Affairs, International Budget Project and the Eastern Regional Organization for Public Administration Interregional Workshop, Manila, Philippines (ST/ESA/PAD/SER.E/94).

more holistic approach so that civil society organisations can participate in various levels of policy-making.

4.2 Sensitising Civil Society Stakeholders

Society includes many stakeholders, of which civil society is one. In a report entitled, 'Civil Society and Other Stakeholders, Leaving No one Behind When Implementing the Agenda 2030', The United Nations identified nine key stakeholders in society that were critical for sustainable development.[r] The report stated that:

> "The outcome of the 1992 United Nations Conference on Environment and Development, NILO, A. November 2015. 3 "Agenda 21" recognized nine key sectors of society or "major groups" as the main channels through which citizens and people could organize and participate in sustainable development processes. These include women, children and youth, indigenous peoples, non-governmental organizations, local authorities, workers and trade unions, business and industry, the scientific and technological community, and farmers"

Civil space existswithin the functioning of civil society and includes aggregate NGOs, extrajudicialinstitutions, public-interest forums and welfare agencies. However, not all stakeholders are equally responsive towards societal issues due to a number of constraints (i.e. financial, faith/religious, class and hierarchy within the society). They should reach out to each other within-the-group and between-the-group in a multi-lateral manner to interact with the local, provincial and central authorities of administration, judiciary and enforcement. The initial stage would be the creation of a knowledge-based central repository where lateral and vertical integration with policy formulation, implementation and monitoring would be possible. This would improve self-accountability and hold authorities and governments responsible for civil society participation.

4.3 Inclusive Functionality

One of the central roles of civil society is to facilitate inclusivity of the democratic process. In a call-out report called 'Civil Society is Central to Inclusive Development', the International Service for Human Rights, an independent NGO,stated that:[s]

---

[r] https://sustainabledevelopment.un.org/content/documents/9486ANilo%20Civil%20Society%20&%20Other%20Stakeholders.pdf

[s] http://www.ishr.ch/news/civil-society-central-inclusive-development

"It is essential that the principle of partnership with civil society as well as the space for civil society to freely operate are at the heart of the post-2015 framework. As the UN Secretary-General unequivocally stated in his report 'The Road to Dignity by 2030', participatory democracy, free, safe and peaceful societies are both enablers and outcomes of development"

The Indian government and civil society organisations have undertaken several initiatives, including the National Rural Employment Guarantee Act, Universal Education Scheme, Rural Regeneration, Environmental Development Schemes, Disaster Management Schemes etc. However, most of these engagements were limited by their scope and scale. Wada Na Todo Abhiyan, a platform claiming to have more than 4000 civil society organisations and individual participants, expressed alarm over the current government's initiatives.[t] Inclusive functioning between the government and authorities remains unfulfilled. Since the mediating role of civil society needs to be strengthened, the inclusive functioning of civil society in policy-making is warranted and should be strategic. Without the participation of civil society, key reforms undertaken by the government (i.e. Make in India, Beti Bachao, Swachh Bharat Aviyanand Demonetisation) would not be credible among the public as the message would be hard to propagate and could be seen as mere rhetoric or political agenda. The policy-making behind these initiatives is excessively bureaucratic and centralised, therefore policy-makers involved with the policy framework need to incorporate more extensive consultations and collaboration with civil society organisations.

4.4 Welfare Optimisation

To maximise welfare, the government should recognise the aggregate preference of individuals and provide practical outcomes that deliver positive change. In the Indian constitution, Article 41 proposes effective provisions for work, education and employment rights; however, India is yet to be termed as a welfare nation as it is severely limited by its random and arbitrary welfare system. For India to have a better welfare system, constructive and concerted efforts must be made using wider democratic means. Firstly, social choices should be studied, and deterministic valuation must be assessed. Secondly, resource availability and allocation must be established. Finally, non-randomised and reform-specific measures must be taken. The entire process involves multi-level assignments and involves the public, the government and administrative and judiciary mechanisms. The government

[t] http://www.india.com/news/agencies/governance-inclusive-growth-not-modis-agenda-civil-society-2165928/

must include civil society organisations to identify priority-based aggregate public preferences. These organisations understand and represent marginalised sections of society that require the most attention. They can also challenge and influence public policies and negotiate on behalf of the people. However, a feature article published in the Indian national newspaper, The Hindu, stated that:[u]

> "In May 2015, a host of civil society organisations wrote an open letter to the Prime Minister of India. The opening paragraph said: "We write to you, as members and as representatives of civil society organisations, and above all as Indian citizens, to express our deep concern on how civil society organisations and their donors are being labelled and targeted. Funds are frozen, intelligence reports are selectively released to paint NGOs in a poor light, and their activities are placed on a watch list. NGO projects have been shut down, donors are unable to support work, and there is an overall atmosphere of State coercion and intimidation in the space of civil society"

This highlights how civil society organisations in India are discriminated against and how they struggle to help with welfare optimisation. The letter continued:

> "Our work for the poor and the marginalised might involve questioning and protest decisions taken by the government, and this is our right. The government may not agree with what our policies are, from opposing nuclear power plants to campaigning to the right to food. Yet we expect the government to protect our democratic right to protest without being targeted as anti-national"

The open letter emphasised the violation of two democratic rights by the government: the right to freedom of expression including the right to protest and the right to form associations.

4.5 Joining Executive, Judiciary, Media and Legislative Parallax

The democratic process depends on legislative, judicial, executive and media functions. To realise ground-level reality, these functions must work congruently and serve the constitutional and extra constitutional interests of their beneficiaries. Civil society plays a role in bringing them together and converging their diverse perspectives into a more cohesive form. Specifically, civil society organisations can successfully enhance capacity building in the public sector through social mobilisation. Democratic functions in India are often segregated and work divergently; for example, legislative proclamations

[u] http://www.thehindu.com/todays-paper/tp-opinion/the-big-squeeze-on-civil-society/article19311070.ece

are often challenged in the judicial system. Judicial decisions are ignored by the political agenda, and media are libelled by the executive branch while the administration is confronted by the media. Such conflicting tendencies breed non-accountability. Civil society organisations can play a mediating role through social audit and they can help to combine the functions so that, although there are differing approaches, common public objectives are honoured and issues are settled. A well-functioning welfare society needs continuous reforms, and one way to achieve this is through the participation of civil society. Civil society organisations can design and monitor the reform process undertaken by the executive, judicial, media and legislative outfits.

4.6 Symbiotic Faith

Religion and faith have a sizable influence on people and country. India is traditionally a multi-faith country with a secular disposition under the constitutional mandate. Religion can be constructive as long as it is meant for civic participation and self-refinement. Beyond that, religion turns into zealotry and behaves in a reactionary way leading to radical frictions. A study published by the British Humanist Association (BHA) UK revealed that the conventional wisdom of endorsing religion as a force that creates better civic engagement is not true, but rather it is a mistaken idea to advance the 'Big Society' advocated by religious institutions and leaders.[v] The BHA Chief Executive Andrew Copson commented that:

> "These statistics clearly demonstrate that having no religion is no barrier to civic participation and volunteering, exploding myths that religious people contribute more to civil society than others. Many aspects of the Government's 'Big Society' agenda are geared specifically towards including and praising the contribution of religious people and institutions. It would far better be properly secular, inclusive and aimed to recognise the real contribution of people regardless of belief"

India is a secular country; however, the country currently carries an unscrupulous undertone that is sheltering sectarian religious propensities. This, in turn, breeds intolerance and defies the core principles of religion (i.e. peace, harmony, cohabitation, kindness and fellowship). A liberal and tolerant approach to different religions and partisan faiths should serve the social space as a common construct. Civil society organisations in India are aware of this and can help affirm people's ethno-cultural identities. The barriers to understanding religion stem from cultural ignorance, limited education and

[v] https://humanism.org.uk/2011/09/22/news-899/

self-moralism. Civil society organisations can help redefine this understanding in an incremental way through various social movements. However, the current government's approach seems unfriendly towards civil society organisations, particularlyNGOs. A report written by the DirectorGeneral of Policies, Policy Department of the European Parliament, entitled 'Shrinking Space for Civil Society-The EU response', states that

> *"Indian government has tightened authorisation requirements for NGOs receiving funding and now forbids them from activities that are not in India's "national interest". The government cancelled nearly 10,000 civil society organisation registrations in 2015"*

4.7 Environmental Commitments

The environmentis one of the key issues that civil society organisations are most concerned about. India has been affected by environmental issues for decades, and these issues largely damage the welfare and well-being of society, either impliedly or explicitly. India currently ranks 141st out of 180 countries in the Environmental Performance Index, 2017, published by Yale University.[w] This performance index identifies core environmental issues and tracks them for 10 years to record their percentage change (Fig. 6.2). Most of the issues were exacerbated as time progressed.

An article published in CNN Travel also indicated that the environment in India wasmassively degrading. In the article, Seema Javed, Senior Media Officer at Greenpeace India, reported that[x] 'being one of the fastest growing economies of the world, we face an "enormous uphill task" of saving natural resources in the face of this kind of demand for growth and development'. Furthermore, she also stated that 'the development path adopted by India is neither sustainable nor equitable and it's leading to widespread degradation of environment'.

Civil society organisations, such as green NGOs, have taken significant roles in improving the environment. However, in 2015, the Institute of Development Studies reported that:[y]

> *"The political space for green NGOs in India seems to be shrinking. This is surprising because historically such NGOs have played a significant role on many landmark decisions around environmental policy. The law of Municipal Solid Waste, battery waste, electronic waste as well as other environmental legislations were all a result of the judicial activism by environmental NGOs"*

[w] http://epi.yale.edu/country/india
[x] http://travel.cnn.com/mumbai/life/cnngo-asks-greenpeace-what-ails-india-656173/
[y] http://www.ids.ac.uk/opinion/green-ngos-in-china-and-india-surprising-developments

Name of indicator	Score	Rank	10 Year change
Health impacts	51.51	134	7.94%
Air quality	28.07	178	−21.59%
Water and sanitation	64.39	126	13.56%
Water resources	48.41	101	0%
Agriculture	51.96	136	−38.13%
Forests	74.80	31	0%
Fisheries	34.74	104	−27.78%
Biodiversity and habitat	63.42	135	−2.14%
Climate and energy	67.19	79	0%

Figure 6.2 *The environmental performance index 2017.*

However, these NGOs were more recently portrayed as speed breakers on the road to progress. Last July, a report by the Ministry of Home Affairs identified environmental NGOs as being anti-industry and antinational as they were retarding the progress of the country. Organisations such as Greenpeace and Climate Works were singled out as the major deviants. In January, a Greenpeace activist was prevented from boarding a plane to the UK. She was on her way to address the UK Parliament about human right violations due to land acquisition for coal mining in Madhya Pradesh. More recently, a report claimed that a law on foreign funding to charities was being used to lodge complaints against non-profit organisations that do not agree with government policy.

Civil society organisations can educate locals and mobilise public awareness for a better environment. Moreover, they can initiate policy debates and protect public interests through due process. These civil society organisations hold a trans disciplinary view that feeds into multi-actor and multi-sector engagements. Thus their involvement in policy-making can make the environmental agenda more people friendly and productive.

5 CONCLUSION

The relevance of civil society in India is becoming increasingly important. The state and government are changing, and reform is central to the process. The government is now characterised by reconceptualisation, and it is seeking collaboration and consultations with all stakeholders of society. However, there is no evidence that people are receiving the expected benefits, and the dynamics between state and civil society are not yet clear. The prospect of aggregate welfare has been questioned. India has made a tryst, and the time has come to redeem and pledge; it seems the development India once dreamt of decades ago has yet to be achieved. A civilised society with social equality is the new concept of civil society and the key to democratisation. India may be on the path to a sensitised and responsible society with altruistic and aware individuals; however, it is not yet free from its internal strife, elitism, corruption, class and caste hierarchy and disparity. Beyond its institutional dimension, Indian civil society has developed to be rational and has demonstrated resilience when addressing social issues. Civil society has largely influenced the socio-economic setting through participatory representation amidst challenges and turbulence. Public interest causes are prioritised by civil society engagements and are supported by social movements. Civil society in India, as a new norm, is responsive, independent and emerging with a sense of renewal from its colonial past. Civil society organisations have created social space for Indian society and gone beyond the conventional centralised form of government; however, civil society only offers a limited overture to the public's entitlements and benefits. The government and civil society in India should work closely together to rise above the narrow confines of the past.

REFERENCES

Ali, A., 2001. The evolution of the public sphere in India. Econ. Polit. Wkly. 36 (26), 2419–2425.

Berglund, H., 2009. Civil Society in India: Democratic Space or the Extension of Elite Domination? Working Paper. Stockholm University, Stockholm.

Singh, V., 2012. An analysis of concept and role of civil society in contemporary India. Glob. J. Hum. Soc. Sci. 12 (7).

CHAPTER 7

Socioeconomic Reforms and Responsive Government: An Indian Perspective

Suraksha Gupta

Newcastle University London, London, United Kingdom

1 INTRODUCTION

The complexities of these socioeconomic issues, with challenges such as corruption and terrorism, have been detrimental to the growth of developing countries such as India. Corruption in a country points towards unethical and irresponsible practices in the public and corporate sectors. The responsible management guidelines require national ecosystems to focus on innovative policies and activities that support and engage different stakeholders (i.e. local companies, local governments, educational institutes, research organisations, media, not-for-profit organisations, civil society and consumers) in socioeconomic development. The success of an initiative to bring about a socioeconomic reform also requires a well-connected business ecosystem, which is difficult to build in a corrupt environment. A well-connected business ecosystem requires support from different institutions such as central and local state governments and financial institutions (i.e. banks, funding bodies, venture capitalists, investment bankers, universities or not-for-profit organisations), which are engaged in research as their core activity. Such an ecosystem breeds innovation capability with support towards the protection of intellectual property. These kinds of capabilities enable both large corporations and small firms to use them as competitive tools to create new markets, recover costs, improve standards, develop new resources and become averse to the risks involved. However, the exploitation of control, levied by government policies enforced on corporations by administrators, has led to high levels of corruption. Such immorality in the environment ultimately leads to bigger problems for governments, such as the perceptions of being unethical, ineffective and irresponsible. As a result, motivating corporations to become engaged in developmental initiatives becomes difficult for the government. Technology is a tool that can facilitate the eradication of corruption by engaging stakeholders in the public, private and academic set-ups.

The introduction of a revised tax structure and format in India on 1 July 2017 was another reform that transferred the responsibility of taxation from origin to the delivery level and included benefits at the consumption level. The aim of implementing a common goods and services tax (GST) was to create an indirect federal sales tax, which would work as a single unified tax system. Implementing the GST at the state and central level has created complications for administrators as it has increased the costs related to compliance for both levels of government. The system of GST assumes that it will reduce the price paid by consumers, reduce the number of indirect or hidden taxes, increase transparency and reduce the opportunities for corruption in the current taxation structure in India, thereby reducing inflation, reducing tax evasion, boosting GDP and increasing the tax revenues of the government. A survey conducted by the OECD revealed that although taxation-related reform in India has narrowed the country's account deficit, it has increased the corporate sector's compliance with regulatory laws and increased financial inclusion.

The Indian government has promoted financial inclusion in various innovative ways, such as introducing a unique identification number, known as an Aadhaar number, for each individual. This unique identification number has given many people access to facilities and services (i.e. banking services) or the ability to claim domestic gas subsidies or obtain a telephone connection, which has created innovative opportunities for them to lead a better quality of life. The OECD report found that, as a result of the Aadhaar number-based identification, 276 million Indian citizens have opened a bank account for the first time since 2014.

Integrating India's innovation and technological capabilities with science through investments in productivity and efficiency for overall well-being will require strategic international collaborations between different agencies and actors, including corporations. An increase in innovation activity and awareness will increase competitiveness in the market and facilitate economic growth and well-being. Overall well-being, when linked with the growth of a developing country such as India, requires pro-poor initiatives that provide equal opportunities to all. Novel innovation in value creation and distribution in the Indian ecosystem exists in two forms: (1) for consumers and (2) for businesses (as novel methods of production, processes and management practices). Universities have innovated reform of the education system and corporations are users of education and implementers of innovation for consumers.

2 SOCIOECONOMIC CHALLENGES: ENGAGING CORPORATIONS

Despite inspiring economic development and encouraging GDP post-independence, India is currently grappling with multi-faceted social issues. Numerous cases of communal rapes or deaths due to issues such as landfill collapse, reflect the lack of respect for human spirit, dignity and life in Indian society. Policymakers in India struggle with issues such as foreign exchange reserves and external debt when trying to establish the country's international positioning, while the majority of the local population suffers from socioeconomic issues such as poverty, hunger, insecurity, mortality, poor sanitation and hygiene, lack of medicine availability and poor quality food. In such a scenario, the leaders in India focus on sustainable development goals (SDGs), thus indicating that initiatives and action plans of all the stakeholders will be directed towards making the world a better place to live by promoting peaceful and inclusive societies, by changing the mindset of its population and by influencing the social environment of the country. Regulations that demand that corporations make a contribution of their revenue towards corporate social responsibility initiatives reflects the approach towards responsible management that has been adopted by the Indian government. Another way to enforce accountability within the corporate sector is through the promotion of public–private partnerships. Considering the diversity of social issues in India, pushing social development through the engagement of corporations requires the incorporation of ethical and responsible initiatives that are macro in nature (i.e. developing infrastructure to generate opportunities of wealth creation) and micro in approach (i.e. changing individual behaviour and thinking by studying cognitive and emotional requirements) (Boatright, 1999; Gupta et al., 2013; Schwartz and Carroll, 2003). A combination of these two approaches (i.e. macro and micro) requires the government to create accountable action plans that will perform regulatory reforms in a creative and inventive manner by applying a national system of innovation.

3 NATIONAL SYSTEM OF INNOVATION

The national system of innovation connects science, technology and innovation capabilities in a manner that can bring prosperity through the creation of shared values in the form of knowledge, employment and health for wealth. As explained by Freeman (1995), the national system of innovation involves activities and interactions in a network of institutions (in both the public and private domains) to initiate adoption, modification and diffusion of new technologies for social inclusion. Simultaneously, other scholars who have discussed the national system of innovation reflect on the active absorption of knowledge using technology and the creation of learning opportunities for everyone through the development of technology-based capabilities. Knowledge is driven by scholarship, and innovation is driven by competition; however, technology makes both knowledge and innovation applicable to the market by making shared values market-driven and by being of benefit to every stakeholder. Therefore, developing countries require innovative approaches to address challenges and overcome the constraints they face. The institutional void in developing countries encourages the corporate sector to participate in the country's progress by implementing strategies that bring about social changes in society. The national system of innovation facilitates the adoption of pro-poor strategies that use advanced technologies to engage stakeholders in a way that promotes social inclusion at the grassroots level. The ability of the corporate sector to incorporate technological advancements in creating value for all stakeholders is a recognised strategy. Value for all stakeholders, when created by corporation linkages developed for business purposes, leads to knowledge transfer that is beneficial for all stakeholders participating in initiatives to combat social issues. Use of the national innovation system in India has enabled industries to invest in technological advancements, commercialise them by coordinating with different stakeholders and utilise them by developing strategic capabilities as solutions for specific social problems (i.e. micro-financing). These success stories indicate that systemic stakeholder engagement of civil society, the private sector and other stakeholder communities can create new pathways for achieving commercial and developmental objectives. The role of public–private partnerships in the field of education and health has also demonstrated how corporations can push national priorities as strategic plans for the diffusion of technology-based instruments.

4 INFRASTRUCTURE, INDUSTRY AND INNOVATION

The focus of the Indian government is to create shared values by raising the socioeconomic status of the country through initiatives such as 'make in India'. The strategic objective of this programme has been to ensure that India is engaged in the global supply chain by promoting India as a manufacturing and research hub to the rest of the global economy. The objective was established based on the assumption that such a position would positively influence domestic business. The success of this initiative involves inviting direct foreign investment into the country for the building of industrial infrastructure. Investments offered by companies from the developed markets, in terms of outsourcing their manufacturing business for global consumers to local firms in India, are expected to improve the business culture of Indian firms through their advanced management techniques. Another objective of the 'make in India' programme floated by the Indian government was the improvement of the job market for the local population and the creation of skill development opportunities for unskilled individuals through companies that provide special training for vocational assignments. Vocational training increases the demand for support in the form of incubation centres offered by corporations for grassroots innovations, as they are different from mainstream innovations. The difficulties faced by grassroots innovations in India are that neither the innovators nor the institutions are equipped to handle their scalability to commercial levels by testing them for proof-of-market concepts. Therefore, engaging industry for the commercialisation of innovations requires design and technological inputs. Large corporations can transcend such support using the technological, human and physical capital available to them. Such developments increase problems such as the movement of populations from rural to urban areas, which makes urban areas unhealthy, polluted and overpopulated. To address the complexity of the 'make in India' initiative, the Indian government combined it with different initiatives such as 'digital India', 'skill India' and 'smart cities'. The 'digital India' initiative enabled Indian companies to have real-time access to institutional services (apart from facilitating electronic banking facilities) through online and mobile platforms. At the same time, the 'skill India' initiative pushed the availability of employees with skills that were relevant to the industry. The objective of the 'smart cities' initiative was to handle issues related to population migration in major cities for employment purposes. To create smart cities with basic infrastructure and a clean environment for a better quality of life, the government invited smart and innovative solutions based on technological advancements as catalysts for social change. The government focused on using technology-based smart solutions for redeveloping and retrofitting the built environment. They also used new layouts and designs to enhance the utility and green-field development of vacant areas using innovative facility planning, including affordable housing, assured water and electricity supplies, sanitation, solid waste management, efficient urban mobility and public transport, e-governance, safety, security, health facilities, educational institutions and employment opportunities.

5 ENERGY FOR ALL

Providing energy for all by the end of 2019 is an ambitious goal set by the Indian government. The country is still facing challenges with the power supply quality due to frequent power outages. These challenges affect the industrial activity, particularly in the manufacturing sector, as they affect the productivity and efficiency, increase the cost of production and discourage domestic and foreign investments. Lack of consistency in the electricity supply is caused by factors such as the cost of the electricity tariff. Due to subsidies provided by the government and loops in electricity distribution at different levels (i.e. regional and state), energy producers are generating electricity at a higher cost and supplying it at a much lower cost. As a result, the entire energy supply chain has been running at a loss for years. A possible solution to these problems is for the corporate sector to use adequate technologies, developed with scholarly laboratories in universities, to monitor the consumption and misuse of energy at various points to drive ethical consumption in civil society. Another important aspect of managing affordable and clean energy for all will require the government to create an ecosystem that will provide sources of research and development for energy supply innovation to universities. The cross-sectional flow of innovation-based knowledge between corporations, academia and industry can improve the energy supply chain performance in a given institutional, legal and regulatory environment. It is important that stakeholders that act as an interface between the energy manufacturer and the supplier are technologically trained to monitor the electricity supply efficiency and are motivated to control energy availability as a product and its supply in the market. Rural electrification campaigns to promote inclusiveness have led to the electrification of 7108 villages that did not have access to energy.

6 POVERTY REDUCTION

Demonetisation is a process through which the legality of a unit of currency ends on a given date and time, after which it is not considered to be valid in the given territory. In India, demonetisation has helped the government to address the important issue of counterfeit money. Demonetisation was a successful step towards building a cashless economy while reducing corruption. In 2007, the World Bank estimated the amount of counterfeit currency in India to be 23% of its total market. As a result, large numbers of transactions in India were being conducted in cash. The use of counterfeit money also provided an easy route for criminals to launder funds for illegal activities such as drug trafficking and terrorism. The demonetisation act was an attempt to curb such illegal activities and to bring cash currency in the country into accounting books through a proper banking system. Demonetisation increased transparency in the financial setting and led to a decrease in the illegal trafficking of funds. An increase in online transactions created an opportunity for illegal funds, which were available to the public, to be converted into legal funds and thereby contributed to the overall tax revenue of the government. Demonetisation also decreased unfair practices in the education, healthcare and real-estate sector in India. The initiative created problems (i.e. crowded banks and inflation) for common people; however, the decision led to the growth of the Indian economy (by ~7%) in the last quarter of 2016. Such government reforms are boosting inclusive growth in India; for example, technological advancements have helped provide access to banking facilities for those who were unable to prove their identity. The engagement of financial institutions has increased the use of innovative methods and allowed the outreach of these facilities to previously deprived populations. The use of biometric devices and mobile technologies for transferring funds has allowed the poor and illiterate population, who did not have previously have access to these services, to perform safe transactions.

7 GOOD HEALTH AND WELL-BEING

Efforts are being made towards ensuring the health of local populations, as their health-related well-being is an important indicator of the socioeconomic development of a country. Although people in India have been struggling with issues related to health and lifestyle, a significant attitude change was noted as people began to be more concerned with healthy eating and lifestyle quality. This led to an increase in the market for health-related products, an increase in the level of infrastructure and facilities in India, changes in the consumption pattern of consumers and marketing strategies of companies and the availability of healthy food. Despite these developments, India still struggles with health-related issues such as mortality in neonates, infants, children aged under 5 years and mothers. Addressing these issues requires a change of attitude towards the physical growth of children. In girls, growth in early years is important to enable the body to handle motherhood before and after birth. Another issue for local governments to simultaneously resolve is the provision of healthcare information and facilities for immunisation against preventable diseases in young children. There are very few skilled individuals who can handle childbirth and provide antenatal care to vulnerable new mothers in rural areas.

Good health and well-being of the Indian population is also related to communicable diseases, such as malaria, dengue and tuberculosis, and non-communicable diseases such as cancer and diabetes. In addition to, the lack of medical education and practices required for promoting good health and well-being, the absence of infrastructure at the district and sub-district level also leads to poor health and lower income. These issues impact the psychological health of individuals earning below a certain income level and increase poverty. The innovative use of technology in both urban and rural areas is helping medical practitioners to monitor the quality of health-related services and medical scholars to collect real-life health data for further research and development. Efforts are being made to use root cause analysis (i.e. business models) and to improve the traceability of the reasons why stakeholders are not engaging in making services and medicines available in remote areas. Indicators included in the healthcare index are helping the government and medical authorities in India to monitor processes used to implement policies. The outcomes of their efforts are being reviewed to find specialty solutions to problems such as generating patient-friendly services, protecting patient's rights at the secondary and tertiary level and providing financial assistance to families of patients earning below the poverty line.

8 EMPLOYABILITY AND ECONOMIC GROWTH

Education and employability skills can transform the lives of people who do not have the resources (i.e. networks or wealth) to push themselves through complicated systems of personal growth in developing markets in which relationships are important for success. Promoting inclusive growth in India requires changing the mindset of the rural population from agriculture-related employment to labour-intensive vocational-based industry sectors that require unique skills. Unemployment makes individuals feel restricted or excluded from certain opportunities; therefore, developing skills related to specific commercial areas tends to reduce social exclusion. The National Skill Development Corporation of India has identified 33 different industry sectors in which to develop meaningful and industry-relevant vocational skills-based courses to be offered to millions of poorly educated people. One of the initiatives taken up by the Indian government is the allocation of a higher percentage of the budget for establishing institutions of excellence (i.e. polytechnics and industrial training institutes) and promoting tertiary education.

The purpose of setting up highly reputed Indian Institutes of Technology, National Institutes of Technology and Indian Institutes of Management, alongside universities and private institutes, is to expand the availability of infrastructure to improve student enrolment and promote traditional, contemporary and state-of-the-art education.

The skill development programme in India focuses on empowering the youth of India with skills related to handicrafts, hand looms, textiles and health. As predicted by the National Skill Development Corporation of India, the country will need approximately 500 million skilled workers by 2022. Creating such a workforce requires systematic resource planning to impart skills-related training and to increase the number of institutes with quality vocational teachers. Considering the geography of India, support will be required from stakeholders in both the organised and unorganised sections of the education sector. A joint effort from both will promote excellence by building a knowledge economy in India. Institutes offering different skills will provide opportunities for students to select the skills to learn and will also improve the accountability of the institutional set-ups. Achieving the goals of the 'skill India' campaign will require coordination between policymakers and the corporate sector in the form of public–private partnerships. Public–private partnerships can catalyse the simulation-based learning of skills as per international industry standards in both urban and rural areas. The public partner can provide vision while the financial support from the private partner can demonstrate commitment, and the partnership can provide a viable ecosystem for implementing technologically advanced innovative models to achieve the goals of 'skill India'.

9 CLEAN WATER AND SANITATION

A large proportion of the Indian population owns an individual mobile phone but lives in slums without any sanitation facilities and with open drainage that generates both solid and liquid waste around them. Government employees working in offices and schools in India initiated the 'clean India' campaign, which today covers all cities and towns in the country. Figures presented in the OECD report in 2017 highlighted that some regions of India suffer from a lack of basic facilities (i.e. toilets) or social infrastructure; however, the 'clean India' awareness campaign has stimulated the building of 34 million toilets in the country. Although these figures are encouraging, many rural areas still lack basic sanitation facilities. Efforts made under the 'clean India' campaign have led the general public to be increasingly aware of general cleanliness in public areas such as schools, railway stations and hospitals, and sanitation facilities are now available in public and remote areas for hygiene purposes. Many public bodies have invested in building clean toilets, which have reduced open defecation in India and increased awareness about the links between open defecation and human health. It has also improved the innovative management of waste, in both solid and liquid state, in urban and rural areas. The main objective of the 'clean India' campaign was to eradicate open defecation in India before the year 2019 through the construction of individual household toilets and cluster and community toilets. To achieve this goal, corporations working as partner firms will require advanced technologies and will need to coordinate with rural authorities to find innovative solutions for laying water pipelines in remote areas. To achieve its objectives, such an initiative requires behavioural change, awareness and an environment that facilitates the participation of corporations.

10 EDUCATING AND PROTECTING YOUNG GIRLS

One of the main socioeconomic concerns in India is the falling ratio of young women to young men. This ratio continues to become further skewed with a decline in the number of women. The main reason for this problem is female feticide and infanticide, the root cause of which is poverty. Gender discrimination due to tradition, lack of education and uncertainty of the future of a girl after marriage drives the negative attitude towards women in the fabric of Indian society. These factors increase problems such as malnutrition, trafficking and the sexual abuse of young girls. Addressing these issues requires stakeholders to take up social development initiatives and empower their representatives at the grassroots level. It also requires the mobilisation of technologically advanced monitor performance of health initiatives, and fulfilling the requirement for girls to have facilities such as toilets and safe hostels in various settings (i.e. schools). The National Nutrition Mission of the Indian government innovatively engages state-level stakeholders to focus on the nutritional and medical requirements of pregnant and lactating mothers, as well as infants and adolescents. Decentralising the implementation of developmental plans through the use of technologically advanced infrastructure has increased the outreach of the medical authorities. Incentives have motivated grassroots workers to participate in their initiatives. Public–private partnerships have also played important roles in the strategic implementation of government plans to run care facilities for distressed children who are looking for medical or emotional support, shelter or foster care. The use of technologically advanced resources allows innovative methods to design, monitor and inspect processes adopted and followed by the local facility representatives and allows the state to respond immediately and provide foster care to children and vulnerable women. The government has developed hostels that provide shelter, counselling and medical, legal and rehabilitation facilities for women and girls in distress. Apart from these institutional policies, education, skill development and demonstration of opportunities are also included to allow girls and women of all ages to progress in their lives and become self-sufficient.

11 CONCLUSIONS

India has successfully demonstrated its ability to systematically approach innovations by promoting financial inclusion through the diffusion of technology in banking formalities, by increasing public energy investments through the creation of solar energy production opportunities and by generating two dedicated freight corridors (i.e. the eastern and western corridors) and rail infrastructure in the transportation sector. The World Bank is supporting the two freight corridors with railway lines to reduce transportation costs, vehicular congestion and gas emissions using technologies that will bring transformational advancements and modern management approaches. This will only be introduced on electric locomotives and not on a combination of diesel and electric locomotives, which will thereby reduce carbon emissions and energy consumption. Implementation of a national system of innovation will bring together innovation, technology and institutions to engage public sector institutions (with regards to governance), private sector corporations (for proof-of-concept), civil society members (for proof-of-market), technological experts, researchers (for innovation) and academics (for dissemination) to achieve goals such as energy for all, digital connectivity for all, housing for all, sanitation for all, health for all and education for all. Considering India's low per capita income and its ambitious commitment to achieving SDGs through economic, social and environmental care of its people, should focus on initiatives that involve collective effort for inclusive development.

REFERENCES

Boatright, J.R., 1999. Does business ethics rest on a mistake? Bus. Ethics Q. 9 (4), 583–591.
Freeman, C., 1995. The 'National System of Innovation' in historical perspective. Cambridge J. Econ. 19, 5–24.

Gupta, S., Czinkota, M., Melewar, T.C., 2013. Embedding knowledge and value of a brand into sustainability for differentiation. J. World Bus. 48 (3), 287–296.

Schwartz, M.S., Carroll, A.B., 2003. Corporate social responsibility: a three-domain approach. Bus. Ethics Q. 13 (4), 503–530.

FURTHER READING

Bartik, T.J., 2005. Solving the problems of economic development incentives. Growth Change 36 (2), 139–166.

Grimaldi, R., Grandi, A., 2005. Business incubators and new venture creation: an assessment of incubating models. Technovation 25 (2), 111–121.

Gupta, S., Kumar, V., 2013. Sustainability as corporate culture of a brand for superior performance. J. World Bus. 48 (3), 311–320.

Jamali, D., Mirshak, R., 2007. Corporate social responsibility (CSR): theory and practice in a developing country context. J. Bus. Ethics 72 (3), 243–262.

Kollmuss, A., Agyeman, J., 2002. Mind the gap: why do people act environmentally and what are the barriers to pro-environmental behavior? Environ. Educ. Res. 8 (3), 239–260.

Kramer, M.R., 2011. Creating shared value. Harv. Bus. Rev. 89 (1–2), 62–77.

Mitchell, R.K., Agle, B.R., Wood, D.J., 1997. Toward a theory of stakeholder identification and salience: defining the principle of who and what really counts. Acad. Manage. Rev. 22 (4), 853–886.

Néron, P.Y., Norman, W., 2008. Citizenship, Inc.: do we really want businesses to be good corporate citizens? Bus. Ethics Q. 18 (1), 1–26.

Roseland, M., 2000. Sustainable community development: integrating environmental, economic, and social objectives. Prog. Plann. 54 (2), 73–132.

CHAPTER 8

Sectoral Approaches to Skills for Green Jobs in India

Gipson Varghese*, Suraksha Gupta**, Kavita Sharma†
*National Skill Development Corporation, New Delhi, India
**Newcastle University London, London, United Kingdom
†University of Delhi, New Delhi, India

1 INTRODUCTION

Sustainable development induces inclusive and green growth by reducing poverty and inequality (Chatterjee, 2005; Cobbinah et al., 2015; van Vuuren et al., 2017). While GDP growth is known to increase unemployment by failing to create jobs (Stiglitz, 2017; Stober, 2015), an increase in the need for low-carbon activities is increasing the requirement for energy conservation skills (Bowen, 2012; Sooriyaarachchi et al., 2015; Zuhaib et al., 2017). Therefore green jobs have been discussed as an important challenge for the 21st century. The benefits of an environmentally-sustainable environment that creates green jobs can also help to bring about social development in developing countries (Forstater, 2004; Kramer, 2011; Pagiola et al., 2005). However, building a sustainable environment through green jobs first requires improvement in the quality of working conditions, occupational safety and health policies, the availability of skilled manpower and higher wages (Goods, 2011; Peck and Theodore, 2000; Torres et al., 2014). These aims can be achieved by greening the productivity of small and medium enterprises through the promotion of energy efficient operations (Chua and Oh, 2011; Dayaratne and Gunawardana, 2015). Sustainable low-carbon initiatives of small and medium enterprises require social dialogues between different stakeholders in a society, such as governments, unions, employers, not-for-profit organisations and local institutions (Debroux, 2014; Jenkins, 2009). It also requires joint actions between these actors to develop the required skills, support from active labour market policies, opportunities for training, the placement of manuals in work locations and plans for the mobilisation of resources for building a green economy (Cagnin et al., 2012; Heery et al., 2012; Roseland, 2000). The concept of green jobs links skills related to the efficient performance of organisational functions, skills required for conserving energy and adhering to environmental policies (i.e. building

Changing the Indian Economy
http://dx.doi.org/10.1016/B978-0-08-102005-0.00008-3

green infrastructure) and skills required for the efficient management of e-waste (Kevin et al., 2015; López Gamero et al., 2011). However, creating and finding green jobs is critical due to the dynamics of the energy market (in terms of unemployment and missing incentives) (Bowen and Kuralbayeva, 2015; Meyer and Sommer, 2014). Government initiatives for the building capacity of small and medium enterprises (SMEs), assessment tools and technical and cooperation policy advice can create green jobs (Albareda et al., 2007; Altenburg and Meyer-Stamer, 1999; Blundel et al., 2013; Frijns and Van Vliet, 1999; Studer et al., 2008; Ubaldi, 2013).

2 SUSTAINABLE ECONOMIC GROWTH THROUGH GREEN JOBS IN INDIA

Achieving green and sustainable economic growth has been one of the important objectives of developmental planning in India. It has gained further importance due to its ability to counteract economic downturn (i.e. the increased rates of unemployment and poverty) by recognising and meeting climate change obligations. Using renewable energy resources and complying with environmental legislation is considered as a way to mitigate some of the acute socioeconomic and environmental challenges that India is facing (Harris and Yu, 2005; Wagner and Armstrong, 2010). As the 'Make in India' policy provides opportunities for investments in all sectors, it is important to ensure that India follows green protocols. To support such a brilliant and vibrant initiative, the mission of 'Skill India' is to prepare the current and future workforce in India and make India a hub for skilled labour.

Indian leaders are committed to ensuring that skills training provided to the local population, through training partners or skill development centres, matches the requirements for employment and livelihood in both traditional subsistence and market economies. India is one of the 'young' countries in the world with 354.4 million people aged 15–29 and it has become the sourcing hub for a skilled workforce. India has a great opportunity to meet the future global demand if its upcoming workforce is prepared and trained. With this in mind, there has been numerous skill development initiatives implemented by both public and private partners. While the existing 'skilling' bodies are being restructured to perform better in the 'skilling' ecosystem, the National Skill Development Corporation (NSDC) has started an initiative to equip the workforce with skills for the world labour market. This process was initiated through India International Skills Centres, which aim to provide trained manpower to the global workforce.

Future labour supply trends mainly depend on the size of population growth and the size of the working-age population (Bloom et al., 2010; Fougère and Mérette, 1999; Samir and Lutz, 2017). Most advanced countries will face an increase in the size of the working population aged over 55 (Bloom et al., 2015; He et al., 2016; Loichinger, 2015), therefore there is likely to be an increased demand for skilled professionals from India. Moreover, replacement demand is forecast to provide more job opportunities in most advanced countries. These opportunities for young and skilled Indian workers requires individuals to prepare and train themselves to international standards and qualifications.

3 NATIONAL SKILL DEVELOPMENT CORPORATION

The global labour market offers opportunities for professionals in high- and medium-level occupations in the science, engineering, healthcare, business and teaching sectors (Lewin et al., 2009). India requires globally-competitive professionals such as managers, technicians, clerical support workers and service and sales workers in these sectors. It is estimated that medium-level jobs in the global labour market are likely to rise and that skilled individuals could gain those opportunities (Beerepoot and Lambregts, 2015; Ratha et al., 2015), therefore India could become a sourcing hub for skilled manpower. India is trying to prepare a skill-ready workforce that will be qualified and required in the global labour market through the 'Skill India' mission. The NSDC has prepared to meet the national occupation standards and is ready to supply globally-required manpower. This is a great opportunity to link with international players to support the Indian government's initiative to offer the best quality human resources to the world labour market.

For a country the size of India, every effort, big or small, is part of a journey. Achieving its mission to quickly scale-up skill development requires stakeholders to maintain a focus on quality. Developing and managing high national standards in the availability of skilled manpower for the renewable energy sector will involve green construction and transportation and will be complemented by waste management (i.e. soluble water-based, solid or e-waste). India has made positive strides over recent years, and the NSDC has made substantial contributions since its conception and formation. When the NSDC was formed, the conversation on skill development was only nascent, standards were limited, the capacity for skill development was low (particularly in the private sector) and there was no unifying agency that was adequately staffed to coordinate these efforts. Over the past 7 years, the NSDC has infused over INR 1000 crores (approximately EUR 140 million) into the market to create private skilling capacity. This has allowed the NSDC to seed, incubate and support over 200 organisations. The ecosystem today offers around 1800 standardised skill development programmes in sectors as varied as agriculture, textiles, leather, manufacturing, automotive, aerospace and cross-cutting areas with a focus on green jobs and persons with disabilities, and has reached close to 10 million trainees.

Through participation in the WorldSkills programme, strong advocacy campaigns, special industry initiatives and projects focused on special areas and disadvantaged groups, the NSDC is also aspiring the young to take-up skilling and extending its reach to underserved and unserved populations. The NSDC is also the implementation partner for the Prime Minister's Skill Development Scheme, which aims to target 10 million young people in the next 4 years through subsidised training costs. Looking to the future, the major focus areas should be:

- Developing a world-class skill development organisation with adequate capacities and capabilities to deliver on the large mandate, which would mean that the NSDC could continuously seek to partner with the best institutions in the world.
- Working closely with states to converge standards and deliver value to the end customer (i.e. the young person looking for the right skill set).
- Enhancing collaboration with industry at multiple levels and generating a separate unit to focus on these efforts within the NSDC.
- Working with international partners to devise best practices and standards and customising these to suit the Indian environment.
- Using measurement techniques to understand the impact of skill development (e.g. the impact of skilling programmes on the cognitive abilities of young people), as this will help India to improve its programme design.
- Increasing the contact with end customers, and extending the relationship with a skilled person beyond the programme to one that continues well into their job.

4 GREEN JOBS AND SKILL DEMAND IN INDIA

Indian policymakers need to ensure that their policies for socioeconomic growth support viable and sustainable strategies for promoting investment in green innovation and infrastructure through the integration of economic objectives and environmental concerns. Integration of these objectives will require institutional support to encourage and promote the initiation of start-ups by the youth through programmes such as ease of doing business, use of IT and ITES. These should facilitate the growth of start-ups, eradicate corruption and provide support for creating a business infrastructure for start-ups. The success of these initiatives for green growth will require stakeholder engagement through digital transformation and transparency. These developments, together with companies offering a price reduction for energy-related technologies, are opening the sector to consumer markets. The supply of products based on low-price energies, such as solar, to consumers should create jobs related to the production, supply, consumption and maintenance of energy. This transformation of supply and consumption patterns will convert the economy into a green economy, which will generate green jobs. Institutions should make sure that adequate measures are taken to link planning with strategies for developing skills and training opportunities to match the focus and ambition of their commitments. As India prepares itself for sustainable economic growth and the development of a green economy that will create green jobs, it is equally responsible to ensure the supply of skilled manpower by preparing the current and future workforce to meet the requirements. The following sectors are growing fast and require a trained workforce.

	Sectors	Jobs and skills
1	Manufacturing: vehicle manufacture and related supply chains	• More jobs will be created through refocusing on hybrid vehicles that reduce greenhouse gas emissions • To meet other customer demands (i.e. low costs), electric, biofuels, bio and compressed natural gas (CNG) vehicles are demanded, and companies should focus on reaching that demographic
2	Extractive industries and power production	• There are demands to increase the efficiency and reduce pollution by employing new technologies • Management systems to support the industry would also create new skill requirements, thus resulting in new jobs • As traditional power generation is replaced with renewable energy sources (i.e. wind power, solar photovoltaics, solar thermal, biomass, biofuels, biogas and pallets) these sectors will require new jobs and new skills

	Sectors	Jobs and skills
3	Construction: aimed at developing green and efficient buildings	• Green buildings and green workplaces will require new job profiles and skills • To manage communities towards green efficiency, multi-disciplined community managers are needed • Social media management personnel (i.e. marketing and content writing professionals) will be required
4	Heavy industry: new machine technologies and robotics to replace human labour	• Machine-learning specialists are needed to support this sector • Skilled individuals who can build adaptive algorithms are also needed • Mechatronics will create new workspace areas for humans • 3D and 4D printing technologies to support production will require specialists
5	IT and IT-supported industries	• Individuals who are skilled in cloud and distributed computing • Big data analytics and data mining professionals • Web architecture and development framework jobs • Social media management
6	Tourism and healthcare and medical tourism	• World class hospitals attract tourists who undergo low-cost but successful treatments, therefore higher number of medium-qualified support staff will be required • Natural health treatments (wellness, rejuvenation and alternative medicine) in India attract more people to enjoy the culture, heritage and health care

5 BEST PRACTICES AND THE INDIAN SCENARIO

At conference of parties (COP) 21, the sustainable innovation forum held in Paris in 2015, India declared that it would attempt to reduce the intensity of GDP emissions to approximately 33%–35% by 2030. To achieve its ambitious plans, India adopted several measures related to clean and renewable energy and promoted energy efficiency in various industry sectors. These efforts have enabled Indian industries to lower their emission intensities, particularly in the automobile and transportation sectors, with non-fossil fuel-based energy conservation initiatives being implemented in the building industry. Policymakers are also promoting the use of renewable and clean energy to increase energy efficiency in the development of climate-resilient urban infrastructure.

The non-fossil fuel-based installed energy capacity of India is anticipated to increase to 40% in 2030 from 30% in 2015. The CO_2 emission abatement achieved by India was 94.92 million tonnes of CO eq. per year, from its installed capacity for renewable power 2. India's aims of achieving 175 GW emission by 2022 from its renewable power would lead to a further reduction of 326.22 million tons of CO eq. per year. India's green coverage, with 24% of land in the country covered with forests and trees, demonstrates the progressive outputs of India's national forestry legislation and policies that have successfully transformed India's forests into a net sink of CO_2. Focus on discouraging the diversion of forestland for non-forest purposes to ensure sustainable forest management calls for afforestation initiatives and the regulation of forestland diversion for non-forest purposes so that the Indian government can increase the size of its carbon sinks. The Indian Intended Nationally Determined Contributions (INDC), which was embedded in 1997 Kyoto protocol and encouraged all participants to commit to reducing emissions; the 2007 Bali COP, which engaged developing countries in mitigation actions; the 2009–10 Copenhagen and Cancun COP, which called for collective mitigation actions by developing countries; the 2011 Durban COP, which identified the post-2020 agenda and the Warsaw and Lima COP, have all encouraged developing countries to assume responsibility. These COPs have highlighted that the contribution of India to carbon space and increased global temperature was minimum and that the highest contribution to climate issues came from China, the United States and the European Union.

Despite contributing less to the problem, India was keen to promote low-carbon emissions by pledging to reduce its GDP emission intensity by 2020 when comparing to the levels that existed in 2005. The objective of Intended Nationally Determined Contribution (INDC) is to promote a sustainable lifestyle that is comprehensive with a balanced approach towards developmental equality issues that India is facing in terms of energy, education, health, housing sector and poverty. India aims to focus on climate justice in a way that will protect the vulnerable from adverse impacts of climate change. INDC centres in India strategically promote clean and renewable energy as a resource for energy efficiency, and less carbon-intensive urban centres work on the conversion of waste to wealth.

Their initiatives aim towards the development of a safe, smart and sustainable network of green transportation that reduces pollution and harnesses available resources towards a cleaner and less energy-dependent environment for a stronger economy. These initiatives are expected to contribute to renewable energy technologies by protecting environmental values and contribute to control global warming by improving the quality of air and depending less on fossil fuels. The INDC reflects the responsibility that India has taken on for its leadership performance, while simultaneously opening doors for green businesses and creating requirements for a skilled workforce.

India currently has a total installed capacity of 309,581 MW (309 GW), which includes 214,003 MW from thermal energy, 43,133 MW from hydro energy, 5780 MW from nuclear energy and 46,665 MW from various renewable energy sources. The installed capacity from renewable energy includes 28,419 MW from wind energy, 8875 MW from solar energy, 4325 MW from small hydro energy and 5046 MW from biomass and waste conversion. The Ministry of New and Renewable Energy plans to ramp-up this capacity to 175,000 MW by 2022. Major efforts are also being made to increase solar energy installations under the National Solar Mission. At present, the contribution of renewable energy to the total power sector is approximately 14.83%; however, this is likely to increase to around 40% by 2022. This can only be achieved by establishing large renewable energy projects, mainly solar and wind. The government envisions a capacity of 100 GW from solar and 60 GW from wind, therefore, the upcoming skilled workforce needs to be trained to address these targets.

6 SKILL COUNCIL FOR GREEN JOBS

Renewable energy and sustainable development are the most upcoming fields for meeting future energy requirements and mitigating climate change (Larcher and Tarascon, 2015; Nejat et al., 2015). Considering its national importance, the Ministry of Skill Development and Entrepreneurship has created the Skill Council for Green Jobs (SCGJ), which works to build capacity for green businesses and cutting-edge climate-friendly technologies. The SCGJ was incorporated as a society on 1 October 2015. It is managed by an industry-led governing council that is promoted by the Ministry of New and Renewable Energy and the Confederation of Indian Industry. The SCGJ will act as a bridge between the Indian government and industry to help fulfil the targets related to skill development. The scope of the SCGJ covers the entire gamut of 'green businesses', including renewable energy, green construction, green transport, solid waste management, water management, wastewater management, e-waste management and carbon sinks, and it aims to cover these by aligning industrial needs with best international standards and practices. The SCGJ has therefore been mandated to address skill requirements in the following sub-sectors:

Sector	Sub-sectors
Renewable energy	Wind power
	Solar photovoltaics
	Solar thermal
	Small hydropower
	Biomass, cogen and combined heat and power (CHP)
	Clean cook stoves
	Biofuels, biogas, pellets and briquettes
Green construction	Green buildings
	Green campuses
Green transportation	Electric vehicles
	Biofuels vehicles
	Bio-CNG vehicles
Carbon sinks	Afforestation
	Sustainable forestry management
Solid waste management	Municipal
	Manure and agro residue
Water management	Treatment (energy recovery and reuse): sewage and food industry effluent
	Conservation: water harvesting, check dams and micro-irrigation
e-waste management	Central e-waste management programme

Corporation managers are also finding it harder to incorporate environmental objectives into their business strategies due to the economic implications for their company. However, it is estimated that India has the fourth largest number of renewable energy jobs globally. The International Renewable Energy Agency calculated that India employs 416,000 people through direct and indirect employment in the renewable energy sector. The SCGJ activities are linked to the national missions of Skill India, National Solar, Swachh Bharat and Make in India. Recent studies regarding the skill gap and possible jobs to be created in this sector have indicated that approximately 1.5 million jobs would be created in the renewable energy sector alone by 2022. Considering the requirements of all national missions and the INDC, approximately 15 million jobs would be created in green business by 2030.

7 STRENGTHENING INDUSTRY CONNECTIONS

The SCGJ is working closely with industries in its sector. Detailed exercises have been undertaken to develop occupational maps for each sub-sector and to perform a skill gap analysis. The SCGJ is also making efforts to position its strategy to directly cater to the manpower required in project areas by identifying project locations and training the workforce in and around project areas. Consultations have been made with over 300 industries in different sectors to understand their current requirement and future business plans. Based on the occupational maps, the SCGJ is now preparing various national occupational standards and qualifications packs to impart systematic training in almost all sub-sectors. The SCGJ is participating in various workshops, seminars and exhibitions to understand the manpower requirements of industry.

8 CONCLUSION

As discussed above, green sector planning is an important step towards reducing CO_2 emissions and pollution from industries and other areas. Both public and private entities understand the necessity of a green economy and its importance for economic growth, development and employment generation. The developing world is projected to contribute more to green jobs than the developed world. Favourable policies and declining technology costs have helped Asian markets to increase job numbers. In addition, the increased demand in Asian markets has created employment opportunities in renewable energy that are related to power installation and domestic equipment manufacturing. The solar and wind markets in India have seen substantial activity and growth, and both sectors have employed more than a lakh of individuals. The Indian government's push for 100 GW by 2022 is generating momentum and is helping private sectors to plan accordingly. However, skilling requirements and job creation require both training and educational initiatives to be stepped-up, as green jobs will require expertise to fulfil solar and wind energy installations in both residential and commercial settings. The talent requirement for performing green jobs will be difficult to satisfy without the engagement of corporations. Governance by institutions, with policy frameworks that call for investments in increasing capabilities through the promotion of education and training, will also be required. The next challenge to be faced is the development of occupational maps and standards for green jobs through competence for certification, assessment and accreditation. Skill assessment efforts to satisfy green jobs will create an ecosystem that can help the Indian government improve the quality of life and well-being of its population.

REFERENCES

Albareda, L., Lozano, J.M., Ysa, T., 2007. Public policies on corporate social responsibility: the role of governments in Europe. J. Bus. Ethics, 391–407.

Altenburg, T., Meyer-Stamer, J., 1999. How to promote clusters: policy experiences from Latin America. World Dev. 27 (9), 1693–1713.

Beerepoot, N., Lambregts, B., 2015. Competition in online job marketplaces: towards a global labour market for outsourcing services? Glob. Networks 15 (2), 236–255.

Bloom, D.E., Canning, D., Fink, G., 2010. Implications of population ageing for economic growth. Oxford Rev. Econ. Policy 26 (4), 583–612.

Bloom, D.E., Canning, D., Lubet, A., 2015. Global population aging: facts, challenges, solutions and perspectives. Daedalus 144 (2), 80–92.

Blundel, R., Monaghan, A., Thomas, C., 2013. SMEs and environmental responsibility: a policy perspective. Bus. Ethics. Eur. Rev. 22 (3), 246–262.

Bowen, A., 2012. 'Green' growth, 'green' jobs and labor markets. Available from: https://52.21.52.208/bitstream/handle/10986/3277/WPS5990.txt?sequence=2&isAllowed=y.

Bowen, A., Kuralbayeva, K., 2015. Looking for Green Jobs: The Impact of Green Growth on Employment. Global Green Growth Institute, Available from: https://www.climate.gov.ph/images/GGGI/Looking-for-green-jobs_GRI_LSE_web_PDF.Pdf.

Cagnin, C., Amanatidou, E., Keenan, M., 2012. Orienting European innovation systems towards grand challenges and the roles that FTA can play. Sci. Public Policy 39 (2), 140–152.

Chatterjee, S., 2005. Poverty reduction strategies: lessons from the Asian and Pacific region on inclusive development. Asian Dev. Rev. 22 (1), 12.

Chua, S.C., Oh, T.H., 2011. Green progress and prospect in Malaysia. Renew. Sust. Energy Rev. 15 (6), 2850–2861.

Cobbinah, P.B., Erdiaw-Kwasie, M.O., Amoateng, P., 2015. Rethinking sustainable development within the framework of poverty and urbanisation in developing countries. Environ. Dev. 13, 18–32.

Dayaratne, S.P., Gunawardana, K.D., 2015. Carbon footprint reduction: a critical study of rubber production in small and medium scale enterprises in Sri Lanka. J. Clean. Prod. 103, 87–103.

Debroux, P., 2014. Corporate social responsibility and sustainable development in Asia. Asian Business and Management: Theory Practice and Perspectives. pp. 139–158.

Forstater, M., 2004. Green jobs: addressing the critical issues surrounding the environment, workplace, and employment. Int. J. Environ. Workplace Employ. 1 (1), 53–61.

Fougère, M., Mérette, M., 1999. Population ageing and economic growth in seven OECD countries. Econ. Model. 16 (3), 411–427.

Frijns, J., Van Vliet, B., 1999. Small-scale industry and cleaner production strategies. World Dev. 27 (6), 967–983.

Goods, C., 2011. Labour unions, the environment and 'green jobs'. J. Aust. Polit. Econ. 67, 47.

Harris, P.G., Yu, H., 2005. Environmental change and the Asia Pacific: China responds to global warming. Glob. Chang. Peace Sec. 17 (1), 45–58.

He, W., Goodkind, D., Kowal, P.R., 2016. An Aging World: 2015. United States Census Bureau.

Heery, E., Abbott, B., Williams, S., 2012. The involvement of civil society organizations in British industrial relations: extent, origins and significance. Brit. J. Ind. Relat. 50 (1), 47–72.

Jenkins, H., 2009. A 'business opportunity' model of corporate social responsibility for small- and medium-sized enterprises. Bus. Ethics. Eur. Rev. 18 (1), 21–36.

Kevin, N.M., Munene, Z., Kimani, M.R., Njagi, K.M., Mbagara, B., 2015. Towards green ICT driven economies: assessing the governments' role in green ICT adoption. Int. J. Appl. Innov. Eng. Manag. 4 (3), 120–131.

Kramer, M.R., 2011. Creating shared value. Harv. Bus. Rev. Jan–Feb.

Larcher, D., Tarascon, J.M., 2015. Towards greener and more sustainable batteries for electrical energy storage. Nat. Chem. 7 (1), 19–29.

Lewin, A.Y., Massini, S., Peeters, C., 2009. Why are companies offshoring innovation? The emerging global race for talent. J. Int. Bus. Stud. 40 (6), 901–925.

Loichinger, E., 2015. Labor force projections up to 2053 for 26 EU countries, by age, sex, and highest level of educational attainment. Demogr. Res. 32, 443–486.

López-Gamero, M.D., Zaragoza-Sáez, P., Claver-Cortés, E., Molina-Azorín, J.F., 2011. Sustainable development and intangibles: building sustainable intellectual capital. Bus. Strateg. Environ. 20 (1), 18–37.

Meyer, I., Sommer, M.W., 2014. Employment Effects of Renewable Energy Supply: A Meta-Analysis. Policy Paper No. 12.

Nejat, P., Jomehzadeh, F., Taheri, M.M., Gohari, M., Majid, M.Z.A., 2015. A global review of energy consumption CO_2 emissions and policy in the residential sector (with an overview of the top ten CO_2 emitting countries). Renew. Sust. Energy Rev. 43, 843–862.

Pagiola, S., Arcenas, A., Platais, G., 2005. Can payments for environmental services help reduce poverty? An exploration of the issues and the evidence to date from Latin America. World Dev. 33 (2), 237–253.

Peck, J., Theodore, N., 2000. Beyond 'employability'. Camb. J. Econ. 24 (6), 729–749.

Ratha, D., Yi, S., Yousefi, S.R., 2015. Migration and development. Routledge Handbook of Immigration and Refugee Studies. 1(3). p. 260.

Roseland, M., 2000. Sustainable community development: integrating environmental, economic, and social objectives. Prog. Plann. 54 (2), 73–132.

Samir, K.C., Lutz, W., 2017. The human core of the shared socioeconomic pathways: population scenarios by age, sex and level of education for all countries to 2100. Glob. Environ. Chang. 42, 181–192.

Sooriyaarachchi, T.M., Tsai, I.T., El Khatib, S., Farid, A.M., Mezher, T., 2015. Job creation potentials and skill requirements in PV, CSP, wind, water-to-energy and energy efficiency value chains. Renew. Sust. Energ. Rev. 52, 653–668.

Stiglitz, J.E., 2017. The overselling of globalization. Bus. Econ. 52 (3), 129–137.

Stober, E.O., 2015. Unemployment scourge: rising to the Nigerian challenge. Rom. Econ. J. 18 (56), 181–200.

Studer, S., Tsang, S., Welford, R., Hills, P., 2008. SMEs and voluntary environmental initiatives: a study of stakeholders' perspectives in Hong Kong. J. Environ. Plann. Man. 51 (2), 285–301.

Torres, R., Chang, H.J., Andreoni, A., Kapsos, S., Lee, E., Nübler, I., Sexton, D., 2014. Productive transformation, decent work and development. World Employ. Soc. Outlook 2014 (1), 63–84.

Ubaldi, B., 2013. Open government data: towards empirical analysis of open government data initiatives. OECD Working Papers on Public Governance 22.

van Vuuren, D.P., Stehfest, E., Gernaat, D.E., Doelman, J.C., Van den Berg, M., Harmsen, M., Girod, B., 2017. Energy, land-use and greenhouse gas emissions trajectories under a green growth paradigm. Glob. Environ. Change 42, 237–250.

Wagner, J., Armstrong, K., 2010. Managing environmental and social risks in international oil and gas projects: perspectives on compliance. J. World Energy Law B. 3 (2), 140–165.

Zuhaib, S., Manton, R., Hajdukiewicz, M., Goggins, J., 2017. Attitudes and approaches of Irish retrofit industry professionals towards achieving nearly zero-energy buildings. Int. J. Build. Pathol. Adapt. 35 (1), 16–40.

FURTHER READING

Poschen, P., 2017. Decent Work Green Jobs and the Sustainable Economy: Solutions for Climate Change and Sustainable Development. Routledge.

CHAPTER 9

India's New Bilateral Investment Treaty: Expansions, Inclusions and Exclusions

Geethanjali Nataraj*, Anjali Tandon**
*Indian Institute of Public Administration (IIPA), New Delhi, India
**Institute for Studies in Industrial Development (ISID), New Delhi, India

1 INTRODUCTION

Globally, countries remain interested in foreign investment as a source of capital for domestic growth and development. The host countries facilitate foreign investment through national investment policies, which include liberalisation and promotional activities at both the national and sectoral levels. Policy measures include sectoral caps, tax incentives, administrative regulations and land ownership. In addition to the promotion of investment, the host countries also ensure the protection of investment through the signing of treaties, which provide them with a rule-based, predictable and nondiscriminatory environment (UNCTAD, 2017). The partner countries (host and home countries) engage with each other through the signing of a Bilateral Investment Treaty (BIT), which is also known as bilateral investment promotion and protection agreement. The BIT negotiations are designed to address investor concerns, whilst also striking a balance through according regulatory space with the host country. A total of 2950 International Investment Agreements (IIAs) have been signed globally. Approximately nine of every ten IIAs are BITs, while the remaining agreements are Treaties with Investment Provisions (TIPs), which form part of a larger Free-Trade Agreement (FTA) that covers many other issues (i.e. trade and non-tariff barriers).

India's engagement in BITs dates back to 1994 while TIPs were initiated after 2004. Following the global trend for prevalence of BITs in IIAs, India has also developed a few TIPs with Singapore, South Korea, Malaysia, Japan and the Association of South East Asian Nations (ASEAN). In comparison to TIPs, BITs have the advantage of being independent of other issues. Since BITs entail investment-specific rules and regulations, they can be amended or terminated relatively easily. This is in contrast to having to renegotiate an entire FTA while addressing the investment-related issues

Changing the Indian Economy
http://dx.doi.org/10.1016/B978-0-08-102005-0.00009-5

only. Thus countries such as India prefer the BIT route for providing and procuring protection for foreign investment.

Like any other policy arena, policies on the protection of foreign investment have also evolved from the age-old Organisation for Economic Co-operation and Development (OECD) Draft Convention for the Protection of Foreign Property, 1967. The draft was designed to suit the protection needs of capital-exporting countries, such as the UK, Germany, France, Spain, the Netherlands, Switzerland, Finland and Australia, as the early participants of IIAs. However, the proliferation of BITs due to the specific architecture of scope and legality, overlapping obligations and divergent interpretations of similar obligations under differing conditions, has made the international setting for foreign investment protection more complex and contemplative.

A key component of the protection commitment in a BIT is the provision for international arbitration during a dispute between an investor and the host government. However, the increased initiation of disputes by a number of developed countries, in relation to the developing partners, has raised alarms about the skewed nature of the existing BIT framework (Kollamparambil, 2016). International research on the impact of BITs on the magnitude of Foreign Direct Investment (FDI) also remains inconclusive. The number of disputes and settlements has increased dramatically, with the number of settlements through arbitration increasing from 50 cases in 2000 to 608 in 2014 (mostly initiated by investors). India alone has faced 20 legal disputes filed by its investment partners.

This has raised serious concerns for the hosting partners and has led to a review of their existing BIT policy frameworks. Many countries and regional integration organisations have considered revising or terminating their existing BITs, and India is amongst those that have reviewed and revised their BIT. India's new BIT came into effect on 28 December 2015. Treaty termination notices were subsequently served to 57 partners including France, Germany, Spain, Sweden, the Netherlands and the UK, while joint interpretative statements were called for with the remaining 25 partners, including Bangladesh, China, Finland and Mexico. Treaty partners such as Tajikistan, Turkmenistan, the Kyrgyz Republic, Switzerland, Oman, Qatar, Belarus, Thailand, Armenia, the UAE and Zimbabwe agreed to a renegotiation, while the EU and other developed countries were resentful.

This chapter provides a comparison of the previous and current BIT to highlight the future challenges and to suggest a potential way forward.

The chapter has five sections. Following the introductory section, Section 2 presents the global IIA trends and a discussion of India's changing investment regime and BIT trends. Section 3 provides details of the changes in the new BIT 2015. International benchmarking of India's BIT is given in Section 4, which is followed by the challenges for the new BIT and the way forward in Section 5.

2 GLOBAL TRENDS IN IIAs AND INDIA'S BIT

Bilateral investment agreements represent a common approach towards strengthening trade and investment linkages between two countries and providing support for foreign investment. In certain cases, these form part of more comprehensive free-trade and economic agreements, which also cover trade in goods and services. The United Nations Conference on Trade and Development (UNCTAD) describes bilateral investment agreements as 'the most important protection of international foreign investment'. Given the impediments to multilateralism at the level of the World Trade Organisation and the growing scepticism against unrestricted investment liberalisation (especially among poorer countries), bilateral investment agreements have emerged as a preferred option to tackle the regulatory issues surrounding foreign investment. In 2016, there were 2950 BITs and nearly 2363 treaties in force. Of this, TIPs numbered 373 and the number of treaties in force was 310 (Fig. 9.1).

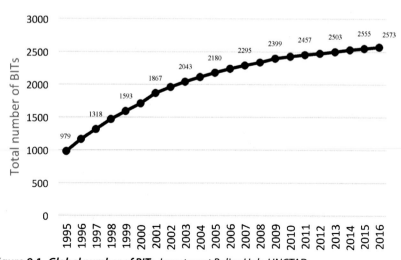

Figure 9.1 *Global number of BITs. Investment Policy Hub, UNCTAD.*

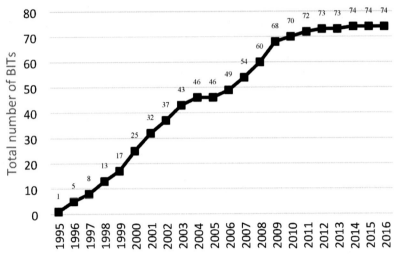

Figure 9.2 *BITs signed by India. Investment Policy Hub, UNCTAD.*

The first Indian BIT was signed with the UK on 14 March 1994. To date, the government has signed BITs with 83 countries, all of which have been negotiated using the model framework of 1993. Fig. 9.2 illustrates the growing trend of India's BITs. However, since 1993 the Indian economy has undergone significant structural change, especially regarding the pace of economic reform and the scope of government regulation. Several major global changes have also occurred simultaneously regarding BITs, particularly the 'Investor State Dispute Settlement (ISDS) mechanism'. The latter represents one of the most controversial elements of India's existing BIT framework.

2.1 Evolution of Foreign Investment Regime in India

The first 20 years of post-independence witnessed moderate levels of regulation and foreign investment in India was received on conditions of mutual benefit with joint ventures as the main corporate arrangements. During the stringently-regulated 1970s and 1980s, a more protectionist approach was adopted; for example, the National Treatment (NT) obligations were applicable to foreign companies with only a minority holding of up to 40%, much to the discomfort of international companies such as Coca-Cola, IBM, Kodak and Mobil (Ranjan, 2017). The government maintained a largely reserved approach towards foreign investment. The benefits of foreign participation became more evident with deregulation of the economy in later years. The success story of Suzuki (Maruti Suzuki)

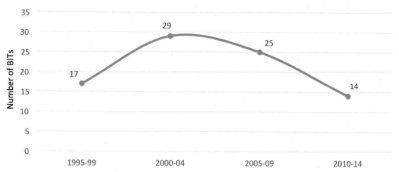

Figure 9.3 *Trends in India's BITs in force.* The number of treaties adds up to 74 as enforcement dates are not available for the other nine treaties. *Investment Policy Hub, UNCTAD.*

in the automobile industry, which replaced the popular Ambassadors and Fiats, has been widely acknowledged. During the high growth periods in the 1990s, the outward-orientated approach also extended to the investment sphere. India has signed many investment treaties since the mid-1990s in a bid to grant additional investment protection. The number of signed BITs increased between 1995 and 2004 and decreased between 2004 and 2014 (Fig. 9.3). As many as 83 BITs have been signed (and came into force) over the 20-year period, and more than half (46) of these came into force by 2004. The decline in BIT numbers during 2005–2009 was not marked, particularly in view of the global financial crisis of 2007–08. However, the notable fall in new BITs during the last 5-year period shows India's cautious approach to investment protection after the first claim was made against India in 2011.[a] This was also a period of review for India's earlier BIT policy of 1993, and since then 17 BITs have been terminated unilaterally, with one termination in 2013, four in 2016 and 12 in 2017 (UNCTAD).

3 THE NEW MODEL BIT: EXPANSIONS, INCLUSIONS AND EXCLUSIONS

The new BIT was finalised after a rigorous 4-year review. The review process was conducted through the constitution of a standing committee of secretaries, which was set-up as an interministerial working group. A draft of the model text was placed for consultations in March 2015, before the final text was approved in December 2015.

---

[a] No BITs were signed after 2014.

The design of the new BIT contained multiple changes. For example, in a fundamental departure from its predecessor, the new BIT introduced the Ministry of Finance (MoF) as the administrative body. The MoF replaced the Ministry of Commerce as the negotiating authority for investment chapters, included in India's FTAs. This major institutional change attempted to consolidate the authority of MoF and aimed to harmonise all investment arrangements either through bilateral treaties or as investment chapters of an FTA.

The new BIT attempted to match the needs of the times through more explicit features. The erstwhile BIT was essentially drafted to suit the interests of a capital-exporting country and had outlived its age. It is important to acknowledge India's endeavour keeping in view its growing outflow of investment. Therefore any changes effective through the new BIT are not only applicable to foreign investment in India only but also influence the Indian investment abroad. This is important to note before commenting on the nature of changes in the new policy. Changes in the new BIT are effective through expansions, amendments or clarifications; inclusions and omissions (Table 9.1). Each of these is discussed in further detail.[b]

Definitional issues are of utmost importance in a treaty. They determine the investments that are eligible for protection and the specific investment agents that are entitled to protection benefits as the subjects of an investment treaty. The shift towards 'enterprise-based' investment in 2015 was a notable change. Under the new definition, investment protection would only be applicable to FDI in India. The switch from the earlier 'asset-based' definition was done to protect investments with relative foothold capital, which are more likely to bring employment and technological and development gains.[c] The earlier 'asset-based' definition extended protection to both tangible (i.e. property, shares and debentures) and intangible (i.e. goodwill and intellectual property rights) assets. Although a wide range of assets remained under protection, those excluded from protection included portfolio investment, government-issued debt securities, goodwill, brand value and market share (Singh, 2016). Operational expenses incurred prior to the enterprise establishment were outside the ambit of protection. Also excluded from protection were issues of taxation, government procurement, state subsidies and local government measures. Other definition changes

---

[b] Refer to Singh (2016) for a detailed review of each clause under the new BIT model.
[c] FDI is generally considered to be a long-term investment compared to the relatively volatile portfolio investment.

Table 9.1 Summary of the changes in India's new BIT model, 2015.

	Features in India's BIT, 1993		Changes in India's BIT, 2015
1	Investment	✓	Calibrated to 'enterprise based' definition
2	Investor	✓	Clarified
3	Fair and Equitable Treatment	X	
4	National Treatment	✓	Qualifiers added
5	Most Favoured Nation	X	
6	Full Protection and Security	✓	Clarified
7	Umbrella Clause	X	
8	Stabilisation clause	X	
9	Expropriation	✓	Case-by-case test approach, explicit statement of non-discriminatory regulatory measures
10	Transfers	✓	Funds for unrestricted transfer listed, with specific provisions for delay/ prevention
11	Investor obligations	+	
12	Investor State Dispute Settlement	✓	Conditional to exhaustion of local remedies
13	Arbitral tribunal	+	Transparency measures
14	Appeals facility	+	
15	Dispute Settlement	+	As an alternate to ISDS
16	Exception clause	+	Scope expanded
17	Provision for review	+	
18	Provision for amendments	+	
19	Provision for termination	✓	Amended

✓: maintained, amended, clarified or expanded; X:excluded; +: included.
Source: Author's compilations based on Singh (2016)

related to the recognition of investors and control; for example, an investor is defined as one who has ownership (direct or beneficial) of more than half of the enterprise's total capital. Enterprise control essentially refers to the appointment powers and decision at a senior management level. The BIT accords protection to an enterprise that is directly or indirectly controlled by an investor.

The removal of the Fair and Equitable Treatment (FET) obligation from the new BIT removed the ambiguity that arose from its interpretation. The FET had a wide but unclear scope due to its unqualified standards. The new BIT addresses the problem by narrowing the scope (without an explicit mention of the FET) through provisions with limited obligations preventing non-denial of justice, fundamental breach of due process, targeted discrimination and manifestly abusive treatment for investing party.

While continuing the NT obligations, the newly attached qualification of 'in like circumstances', although still not explicitly clarified, leaves room for differentiation between investors and their investments.

Another feature has been the exclusion of the Most Favoured Nation (MFN) provision. The MFN clause remains the most commonly used by investors to gain access to protection when treaty shopping. The MFN clause is often used to protect benefits beyond the specific treaty but within the jurisdiction of other treaties.

The new BIT only clarifies obligations relating to the physical security of the investor and investment, perhaps to exclude guaranteed legal security for the investor. The earlier treaty obliged the host state to provide active measures to protect against adverse effects. The definition was broad and was interpreted to include effects such as those from demonstrations, employees or business partners or from the actions of the state and its organisations (i.e. the armed forces) (Schreuer, 2010).

The 'umbrella clause' was excluded because of its controversial nature. The broad language of the provision traditionally permitted the inclusion of numerous types of obligations. The uncertainty arising from the wide scope and nature of the clause provided ambiguity with regards to an investor's ability to challenge a regulation change in the host country. Furthermore, the absence of a stabilising clause in the new BIT has provided room for regulation change related to investment activity.

Regarding the expropriation of investment, the new BIT adopts a case-by-case approach to test if a specific regulatory measure amounts to exportation. Nondiscriminatory measures on account of public interest (i.e. health, safety and the environment) are explicitly noted as exceptions.

A list of eligible funds is available to allow unrestricted transfers while maintaining provisions to delay or prevent insolvency and noncompliance following bankruptcy.

The inclusion of investor obligations mandates that the investment enterprises be constituted, organised and operated while following the rules. It also requires them to follow taxation laws and disclose information for greater transparency.

The new BIT retains the ISDS mechanism as a major protection instrument against the host government; however, international arbitration can only be initiated after exhaustion of domestic remedies. The newly-designed time-bound approach requires the foreign investor to resort to local judiciary before an international arbitration claim can be made. However, the investor can still commence international arbitration, with a prior notice of at least 90 days, if sufficient evidence is available to support unjustified delays. Investment claims can only be raised within 1 year of the measure enforced, and the simultaneous pursuit of settlement proceeding under local and international arbitration is prevented under the new policy.

Strict procedural details are stipulated as part of the arbitral tribunal conduct. The independence of the arbitral procedure is ensured through transparency and discourse statements. The provision for an appellate mechanism is included for a review of the international arbitration award. While maintaining the ISDS, the new BIT has an added State–State Dispute Settlement that encourages mutual settlement. The expanded exception clause now provides domestic policy with space for core issues arising from measures related to welfare, the economy, the environment and society. These are in addition to the security concerns that already existed in the earlier text.

Three more provisions have been included that relate to the review, amendment and termination of treaties. The treaty text has a provision for a quinquennial review, which indicates the openness for the continuous evolution of the BIT policy of 2015. There is scope to amend the treaty at any time during its lifespan. The treaty is deemed to expire after a default period of 10 years after its enforcement (as compared with the earlier period of 15 years) unless renewed explicitly; however, the treaty can be terminated during its course through a 12-month notice period. The sunset clause was retained to prevent investment protection from ceasing (that arrived during the treaty period), with a cover period of another 5 years.

4 BENCHMARKING BIT WITH OTHER IIAs

The new BIT is a major departure from earlier models (1993 and 2003) as it incorporates substantial changes in an attempt to safeguard the interests of the host state. This section attempts to compare India's BIT with model investment agreements from other countries, including the investment provisions included in the Trans-Pacific Partnership (TPP), the EU–Canada Comprehensive Economic and Trade Agreement (CETA), the US–Korea FTA and the India–Korea Comprehensive Economic Partnership Agreement (CEPA).

The first major departure in the new BIT was the adoption of an 'enterprise-based' definition of investment (in place of an 'asset-based' definition), which narrowed the scope of investments covered. It defined an 'enterprise' as:

- Any legal entity constituted, organized and operated in compliance with the law of a party, including any company, corporation, limited liability partnership or joint venture, and
- A branch of any such entity established in the territory of a party in accordance with its law and carrying out business activities there.

The revised definition of investment also excluded portfolio investments, goodwill, brand value, market share and other intangible rights and also implicitly stated that the investment ought to contribute to the development of the host's economy. Conversely, all major IIAs including the US–Korea BIT (2012), EU–Canada CETA (2016), India–Korea CEPA (2009) and TPP agreement adopt the more expansive asset-based definition, which includes every asset that an investor owns or controls (directly or indirectly) including expectations of gain or profit or the assumption of risk.

Another notable feature of the new BIT was the exclusion of the MFN clause, which was intended to counter discrimination among foreign investors. The rationale for exclusion relates directly to the Indian government's loss in White Industries versus The Republic of India case. In this case, White Industries Australia Limited invoked the MFN clause from the India–Australia BIT to benefit from the more favourable investor rights provided in the India–Kuwait BIT to appeal the right for an effective means of asserting claims and enforcing rights. The exclusion of the MFN clause in the new BIT ensures that other countries do not resort to the phenomenon of 'treaty shopping' (i.e. borrowing clauses contained in other BITs).

In comparison, while the investment chapter proposed by the EU for Transatlantic Trade and Investment Partnership (TTIP), and incorporated in the CETA, also limits the possibility of foreign investors taking recourse to agreements with third countries to obtain more advantageous substantive provisions, both the US–Korea BIT and the TPP agreement include a broad MFN clause. The MFN clause is also missing from the investment chapter of the India–Korea CEPA signed in 2009. The Law Commission of India also highlighted the absence of the MFN clause in the model BIT, stating that it would expose investors to discriminatory treatment and that an exception could be made whereby the scope of the clause would be restricted to the application of domestic measures. However, to help easy BIT negotiations with other countries, the revised BIT model added a clause dealing with compensation for losses and nondiscrimination in exceptional circumstances (i.e. during war, conflict, civil unrest and national emergencies).

The new BIT model also failed to extend FET for foreign investors. This is the most commonly invoked treatment standard in the ISDS with the majority of successful cases based on claims of infringement of this provision. The FET generally reflects the minimum standard prescribed in international customary law, while others see it as a separate and more expansive treatment standard. In India's 1993 BIT model, petitioners could approach international tribunals without a preliminary verdict from domestic courts in the host state; however, in the new model BIT, investors must first seek domestic remedies for at least 5 years before approaching international forums. There is also a limit to the power of tribunals for awarding only monetary compensation.

The majority of BIT arbitration is assessed by the International Centre for Settlement of Investment Disputes (ICSID), which has a membership of over 140 countries. The ICSID is currently the preferred institution around the world for the resolution of investment disputes. All member countries are governed by the rules and regulations set forth in the ICSID Convention. India is not a member of the ICSID; instead, it follows an ad hoc arbitration format in most BIT dispute resolution cases using rules from the United Nations Commission on International Trade Law (UNCITRAL). The tribunal is started following consensus of the parties or upon failure to agree by the appointing authority (which can be nominated by the parties or is the Permanent Court of Arbitration). There is an appeal process when UNCITRAL rules are used; however, the ICSID does not provide such a direct and clear appeal option. Therefore there is less institutional control and a perceived sense among parties that they have more control over the arbitration process, the choice of arbitrators etc. (NDA, 2015).

Therefore the decision not to follow the standard ISDS mechanism under the revised BIT framework could affect long-term FDI into India. Conversely, other countries have managed to ensure FET whilst also following the standard ISDS mechanism for dispute resolution. In the TPP agreement, the parties explicitly link it with the minimum standard of treatment under customary international law, whereas the EU proposal for the TTIP (included in the CETA) includes specific grounds to be fulfilled to achieve FET (Kaszubska, 2016). Both the TPP and CETA texts refer to the protection of the investor's legitimate expectations, which is something not included in India's model. However, in contrast, FET is part of the India–Korea CEPA, which was signed before India decided to restructure its existing BIT model.

Finally, the new BIT model raises issues concerning India's approach towards extending investment protection to the pre-establishment stage. One of the major hurdles to the India–US BIT relates to the fact that the United States has requested pre-establishment protection, which implies that investors should be protected even before their investment has been made in the host state. Traditionally BITs from European countries have NT obligations that start only after the investment has been established in the host country; however, the recent EU–Canada CETA includes a pre-establishment phase under the market access and NT provisions. Even the TPP agreement extends its investment provisions to the stage before entry. India's BIT model (including the India–Korea CEPA) does provide NT to investors; however, this treatment only includes de jure treatment, unlike the US BIT model which includes both de jure and de facto NT to investors. The scope and general provisions of India's revised BIT are also far more stringent than other IIAs, which has led to resistance on the part of the United States and EU to negotiate their bilateral agreements with India.

This analysis highlights that there is no uniformity among countries, either developed and developing, as to the level of protection required for foreign investors in host states. Every country or agreement follows its own approach towards investment facilitation and therefore IIAs are increasingly developing in different directions.

5 CHALLENGES TO THE NEW BIT AND THE WAY FORWARD

India's new BIT model introduces a number of progressive provisions (e.g. Article 10 on transparency and Article 13.4 on investments made through corrupt practices); however, it generally constrains the standard of protection provided to investors vis-à-vis India in the existing IIAs.

The EU has expressed concern with India's decision to terminate its current bilateral agreements with individual EU members and the requested renegotiation of BITs with each EU country separately. This goes against the spirit of the EU and is likely to adversely impact European investors in India. The EU does not have a provision to allow its members to negotiate BITs independently, and the EU Trade Commissioner has cited a major legal constraint in concluding the agreements following the EU Lisbon Treaty of 2009. However, given the significant time that would be consumed by the EU in concluding new investment agreements with India, the EU has taken recourse to a transitional solution that gives individual member states flexibility and leeway to negotiate investment agreements to ensure that European investments abroad benefit from the legal protection.

Notably, EU regulations do allow member states to amend their existing BITs and conclude new ones under specific circumstances after obtaining permission from the European Commission. In this context, the envisaged EU–India Bilateral Trade and Investment Agreement, which is expected to include an investment chapter, will stand in the way of individual member states concluding separate BITs with India. In fact, the EU has refused to sign the impending FTA with India and has requested to first sign a BIT with the country. However, negotiations on the BIT are unlikely to move rapidly due to differences in the ISDS mechanism and the exclusion of taxation from the BIT.

The United States has raised similar concerns to the signing of a BIT with India due to the revised framework. There is little common ground between the two countries with respect to the BIT. Contrary to India's BIT model, the US BIT model of 2012 includes MFN, recognises that taxation measures could result in the expropriation of foreign investment, is not limited to an enterprise-based definition of foreign investment and does not require the exhaustion of local remedies before initiating international arbitration (Ranjan, 2016).

It remains to be seen which of the new features of India's revised BIT find a place in the BITs that India seeks to negotiate, although it is apparent that several countries are likely to resist many of the proposed changes. In the event that the model BIT text is adopted between India and certain states, investors are expected to negotiate a specific investment agreement suited to their interests rather than relying on the limited protections contained in the model. Alternatively, investors may restructure their investment through a third state to gain protection from a more favourable BIT, which India has not successfully renegotiated (Allen and Overy, 2016).

Renegotiating its existing BITs is likely to be a tedious, complex and time-consuming task for the government. In addition, the investment chapters in the CEPAs that India has signed with Korea, Japan, Singapore and Malaysia are also a matter of concern. Whether the investment protection measures in these agreements need renegotiating is also a serious matter to these countries. The government is yet to establish a clear stance on these issues (Nataraj, 2016). The revised BIT model makes it clear that India wishes to be the rule-maker rather than rule-taker when rewriting the global trading architecture rules.

REFERENCES

Allen and Overy. 2016. Indian Model Bilateral Investment Treaty. Available from: http://www.allenovery.com/publications/en-gb/Pages/Indian-Model-Bilateral-Investment-Treaty.aspx. Accessed on 3 April 2017.

Kaszubska, K., 2016. Making BITs less biting: India's reform of the investment regime. Occas. Pap., Available from: http://cf.orfonline.org/wp-content/uploads/2016/11/Occasional Paper_101.pdf. Accessed on 3 April 2017.

Kollamparambil, U. 2016. Why Developing Countries are Dumping Investment Treaties, The Conversation. Available from: https://theconversation.com/why-developing-countries-are-dumping-investment-treaties-56448.

Nataraj, G. 2016. Will New BIT Help Promote India's FDI? Here's Why Investments May Get Affected. Financial Express. Available from: http://www.financialexpress.com/opinion/will-new-bit-help-promote-indias-fdi-heres-why-investments-may-get-affected/432526/. Accessed on 3 April 2017.

Nishith Desai Associates (NDA). 2015. Bite of the BIT: The Steady Rise of Bilateral Investment Treaties and a Pro-Investor Regime in the Global Economy. Available from: http://www.nishithdesai.com/fileadmin/user_upload/pdfs/Research%20Papers/Bite_of_the_BIT.pdf. Accessed on 3 April 2017.

Ranjan, P. 2017. Turning the Clock Back. The Hindu.

Ranjan, P. 2016. India Seeks Protection with New Model Bilateral Investment Treaty. The Wire. Available from: https://thewire.in/22423/india-seeks-protection-with-new-model-bilateral-investment-treaty/. Accessed on 3 April 2017.

Schreuer, C., 2010. Full Protection and Security. J. Int. Dispute Settlement, 1–17, doi:10.1093/jnlids/idq002.

Singh, K., 2016. An Analysis of India's New Model Bilateral Investment Treaty. In: Singh, K., Ilge, B. (Eds.), Rethinking Bilateral Investment Treaties Critical Issues and Policy Choices. Both Ends, Madhyam and SOMO.

UNCTAD, 2017. In: World Investment Report. Investment and the Digital Economy.

FURTHER READING

European Commission. 2016. Comprehensive Economic and Trade Agreement (CETA). Available from: http://trade.ec.europa.eu/doclib/docs/2014/september/tradoc_152806.pdf. Accessed on 3 April 2017.

Ministry of Commerce, Government of India. 2009. India-Korea Comprehensive Economic Partnership Agreement. Available from: http://commerce.nic.in/trade/INDIA%20KOREA%20CEPA%202009.pdf. Accessed on 3 April 2017.

Ministry of Finance, Government of India. 2015. India's Model Bilateral Investment Treaty Text. Available from: http://www.finmin.nic.in/reports/ModelTextIndia_BIT.pdf. Accessed on 3 April 2017.

Office of the United States Trade Representative. 2016. Trans Pacific Partnership (TPP) Full Text. Available from: https://ustr.gov/trade-agreements/free-trade-agreements/trans-pacific-partnership/tpp-full-text. Accessed on 3 April 2017.

INDEX

Printed in the United States
By Bookmasters